Dial E
for
Endearment

Heidi Gray McGill

HEIDI GRAY McGILL

Thorne Library,

Thank you for making my college experience richer.

Heidi MVNU '88

I

ASIN:
ISBN: 9798775532499
Imprint: Independently published

Cover design by: Chautona Havig

Printed in the United States of America

For information or to contact the author, please email
Author@HeidiGrayMcGill.com.

Unless paraphrased, otherwise noted or indicated,
all Scripture quotations are from New International
Version. Biblica, www.biblica.com/bible/niv/
Isaiah/49/. Accessed 29 Oct. 2021.

To those who see their disAbility
as merely a challenge to overcome
something others only attempt.

"All the world is full of suffering. It is also full of overcoming."

HELEN KELLER

CONTENTS

INTRODUCTION

Through My Eyes

Everly, the main character in *Dial E for Endearment* and I have something in common, but it may not be what you'd expect.

As Blowing Rock, NC's JOY Radio talk show host, Everly has discovered fulfillment, but she hasn't found love, at least not for her—not even from her mother. Everly wants words--heartfelt, meaningful endearments meant for her ears only. She wants a man who will open her eyes to everything she cannot see to make her feel more than just the voice behind the mic.

You may know me as an author, but did you know I am also the retired Director and Founder of an ESL program, regularly walk 12 plus miles a week, care for my grandsons, scrapbook, read voraciously, cook, and am legally blind? That last phrase was difficult for me to say out loud not that long ago.

Vision loss does not discriminate.

My diagnosis in 2001 of Retinitis Pigmentosa

was devastating. There is no cure. There is no surgery. But that does not mean there is no hope.

I still have value.

Those who do not know me well often don't realize I have low vision. As humans, we are amazingly adaptable, and I do a pretty good job covering up my disability. My friends have learned to watch out for me and alert me to potential pitfalls, some better than others, which is always good for a laugh. I use a cane when I'm navigating alone. I've traveled to China—that cane my only companion.

Being blind is certainly not something I would have chosen, but...

Blindness does not define me.

Join me on this fun adventure and see for yourself that God does not discriminate. You'll laugh your way through mishaps--most of which may have happened to me at some point...although I'll most likely deny if asked. But most of all, you'll learn that we ALL have value, and that includes YOU.

February is Low Vision Awareness Month.

One

Everly

The Devil Made Me Brew It is my favorite blend of coffee. Just the name puts a smile on my face even before the first whiff reaches my nose or sip hits my tongue. Here I sit at Camp Coffee Roasters on the edge of town in Blowing Rock, North Carolina, waiting for love and the steaming brew I am about to consume. Love seems to evade me.

As a radio talk show host who gives relationship advice, you'd think I would have good suggestions for how to meet that special someone. Online? On the air? At church or social functions? Maybe the old-fashioned way -- if that's even possible anymore? Or perhaps a blind date? I surmise I'd have more answers if I were out there in the dating scene myself. The only love relationship I have these days is with a cup of joe. At least he has a decent name.

"Here you go, Evie." Jay, the owner, greets me the same way each morning—full of exuberance, his passion for what he does showing in the smile I know must be on his face because I can hear it in his voice. "What's on the agenda for this lovely Friday morning?" The heavy *clunk* of the hand-thrown mug, followed by the sound of grit on wood as he slides it my way, brings with it a thrill.

Warmth emanates from the baked clay as I slide my hand across the table, entwining my fingers with the smooth glazed handle in a warm embrace. "Mmm." He waits for my response until after I've had my first sip. "I thought I'd stroll Main Street this morning, then visit my mom this afternoon, before heading to work this evening." Liquid sunshine brightens my day with each swallow.

"You'll need more than coffee." Jay knows most of my story, and I'm not sure if he refers to my trek through town or the impending visit with my mother. The sound of his slip-resistant shoes does not match what I expect he wears when he's not working.

"Never underestimate the importance of being properly caffeinated." I lift my mug in a mock salute.

"Yeah, well, the tourists are already here to see the leaves changing." I hear his measured footsteps to my right. "Amanda made pumpkin cookies this morning. Care to try one?"

"If your wife made them, then absolutely." The aroma of pumpkin spice tells me he has one ready to share—the bell above the door jingles before I utter my thanks.

"On the house. Send some tourists our way," he whispers before greeting the new customer.

Familiar fall spices tease my senses. Not usually one to eat something so sinful first thing in the morning, I can't resist. The smile that creeps over my face at that first bite is due mainly to the perfection of the cookie, but also because I cannot help thinking how blessed I am to live in this marvelous town in such a remarkable part of the country.

Just a few blocks up the hill off Main Street, my cozy 1930's bungalow sits nestled amongst sizeable red maple and black gum trees, most likely older than the house and the town. I leave the large un-insulated windows open in the summer to keep the cool breeze circulating the non-airconditioned rooms. In the winter, plastic wrap, packing tape, and heavy draperies keep the chilly mountain air out.

I love my home, my street, and my town. I'm within walking distance of several restaurants and an excellent coffee shop. My weekends are filled with local events, a farmer's market, and a church I attend when I can't get a ride to the one I usually frequent in Boone. Even a grocery store is close, and I often go there when I need only a few items. I Uber everywhere else.

The familiar sound of a satisfied customer sipping his coffee fills my ears. I lift what remains of both my coffee and the cookie. The corners of my mouth join in. "You should try one of these. It goes perfectly with the coffee."

"I might just do that next time. Thanks for the coffee, Jay."

"My pleasure. Tell your wife I said, 'Hi,'" Jay calls to the man as the bells sing their familiar tune. I hear Jay move my way. "I'm glad you enjoyed it, Evie. I'll get that." The *clink* of my mug on the now empty plate catches my attention.

"Thank you. I could have gotten it. And, thanks again for the pumpkin cookie. Tell Amanda she outdid herself this time." Unfolding my red and white cane, I stand and push in my chair before slinging my backpack over both shoulders.

"Will do, Evie. See you tomorrow." The bells jingle again, and I hear Jay's genuine greeting to his new customer.

"See ya," I murmur. Even after all these years without my sight, I still use the common phrase. *Wham!*

"Oh! I'm so sorry. I didn't see you." The exasperation in the man's voice shows his frustration and embarrassment.

"No worries. I didn't see you either." I hear Jay snicker as I head out the door, ready to tackle the day.

"It's always a beautiful Friday night in Blowing Rock, North Carolina. You're listening to JOY radio with host Everly Johnson. We're ready for our first caller. Welcome, Jane. You're on the air. What brings joy into your life today?"

The caller's pause always seems odd to me. Every time I start an interaction on the air, I ask the same question, so it isn't a surprise, especially if they listen to the show each Friday night. I have my reasons for asking. I figure if they focus first on what they are thankful for, then maybe it will cut down on the whining.

"Um, Hi, Everly. I guess the rain. I mean, we've needed it, so that means I don't have to water...."

Still listening to Jane, I motion to Scott, my station manager and best friend, using the all-too-familiar hand signals to let him know I am getting feedback in my headphones. My fingers run across the bar in front of me as I simultaneously focus on the caller's familiar story and cue up a song that matches her circumstances.

"Well, Jane, I sympathize with your situation. Loneliness is a challenging place to be in life. A friend once told me that it is better to be single and alone than married and alone." I pause only long enough for my words to sink in. "I have found my church family to be the best place to find connection and the true love I crave. Immersing yourself into the lives of others will fill you deeply."

"But don't you ever get lonely being single?"

Inwardly I cringe at Jane's question. "I have the perfect song for you, Jane. *Restless* by Audrey Assad reminds us that no matter how anxious our hearts may be, there is rest in God's house and with His people. I encourage you to find a place of worship, someplace where you feel God's presence through His people and hear His words through the teaching. Then, find a way to serve. Turn your sorrow into joy." The first notes of the song accompany my words. "Thank you for your call tonight, Jane. We'll be right back with Christian Singles Advice on JOY radio after this song."

Scott beeps in before I have my hand on my Yeti of chamomile tea. I love coffee, but more caffeine probably isn't a good idea after what I learned during this afternoon's visit with my mother.

"You okay, Everly?" The concern in Scott's voice is evident.

"Sure," I lie through the smile on my face. My time with Mom this afternoon hadn't been what I expected, and I am still struggling. Bringing my problems to work is never a good idea, and I need to get my head on straight. Scott reads me like a book, one with plenty of dogeared pages.

"Well, these flowers might help."

He must be holding them up since I hear Walt

telling him to be careful not to spill the water on the equipment.

"Expensive bunch this time. No carnations."

No doubt, the arrangement came from Bless Your Heart downtown. The man is clueless. I can no more see what Scott is holding than I can see the future.

"Thanks, Scott. I'm sure they are lovely. Put them in the break room, and I'll take them to Mom in the morning."

"Want me to read the card?"

I imagine Walt shaking his head as I hear him whisper, "Seriously, dude. No wonder you're single."

"That's okay, Scott. Thanks though. Time to get back to our callers. Do you have another lined up and ready?" I interrupt, already knowing the answer.

"Marcus from Boone. Sounds like a college student." Scott says his familiar 3, 2, 1 in my headphone to let me know I am on the air.

"I'm so glad you could join us on this rainy Friday night, Marcus. What brings joy into your life this evening?

"Am I on the air? Hello?"

"Happy Friday evening, Marcus."

"Well, uh, okay, um…."

There is always at least one of this type of caller on the show each Friday evening. This guy hasn't planned out his thoughts and needs some assistance.

"Marcus, what one thing brought you joy today?" I repeat my familiar phrase.

"Oh, yeah! So, I hung out with these friends after class today. And there's this girl. She's, she's...."

Again, I help him along. "Smart? Funny? Kind?"

"No. She's deaf." I detect a chair squeak in the background. "And, I mean, yes."

"Yes?" It's like pulling teeth getting information from this guy.

"Yes. I mean, she is super smart, funny, kind, and..." he pauses slightly, "she's smokin' hot."

It takes effort to keep from laughing, but I school my features. I know my facial expressions come across the airwaves through my voice. I place a practiced smile on my face before answering.

"Marcus, she sounds lovely. Are you thinking of asking her out?"

"I don't know. What would we do? Where would we go?"

"Just because she's deaf doesn't make her different from a hearing person. I'm guessing that if she enjoyed your time together this afternoon, she might be willing to do something fun with you. How about a walk? You know, Moses H. Cone Memorial Park is one of my favorite places to hike." I shouldn't have said that on the air. Remaining anonymous is hard, and small bits of information are like fuel to some people's fire.

"Yeah! That might be fun. Or maybe kayaking. She likes stuff like that."

I listen as Marcus works through options for their potential date and marvel at how often in my life I've wished for someone who would see past the white cane I carry. I must have daydreamed a moment too long, for I hear Scott's tap in my headphones.

"Marcus, it sounds like you've got a great plan. Thanks for calling in tonight, and I wish you the best." I end the call and immediately pick up the next.

"You are on the air, Bill. Can you share with our listeners something that brought you joy today?"

"Hi, Everly. Yes, today was full of joy. My daughter delivered my first grandson this morning." I hear what sounds like a tissue braising the mouthpiece of his phone. "She named him after my dad."

The quick intake of breath and rise in the tone of the last word confirm my suspicions: Bill is emotional. Tears on the air can be a challenge. An emotional caller often gets loud, or their words take on a high-pitched tone, making listeners uncomfortable. The balance of keeping listeners interested or choosing to change the channel is tough. I make a quick judgment call.

"Oh, Bill. Congratulations! Babies are a gift from God. How are mommy and baby doing?" It's a tricky question, but I pray all is well, and his tears are tears of joy.

"Great. Just great." Bill hesitates only slightly. "I'm actually calling because I have a question for you."

"That's what I'm here for, Bill. Ask away."

"I'm single. Widowed, actually. I'm an engineer who makes good money, and friends say I'm decent looking, but I can't seem to find a good Christian woman I enjoy spending time with."

"Bill, you are not alone. Making connections with other Christians takes effort. You just be you and, if it's God's will, the right woman will come along. I have a song that fits this situation perfectly; *You Are Loved* by Stars Go Dim. It's one of my favorites and reminds me that my Heavenly Father loves me."

"Thanks, Everly. You wouldn't be interes...."

I cut off Bill's question before he has a chance to finish. I know what he's getting ready to ask. At least once a week, I receive a request for a date, or get flowers, or receive candy from an interested suitor.

Spending time with callers both rejuvenates and drains me. I crave the connection I receive from the public yet strive not to take on the caller's burden. No matter how I feel, I portray the happy and ful-filled single talk show host. Some would say I'm not qualified for such a position, and that might be true. I'm not a psychologist or mental health worker. I'm just me—a single girl with a Communications Degree and Psychology Minor who wants to help people.

Don't get me wrong; I do have some experience. I've had my fill of relationships, crushes, pity dates, and broken hearts. To be honest, I rarely give advice. With a bit of prompting and a few well-placed questions, callers often find their own answers. Most likely, they've known them all along. Still, no matter how much I help others, my own issues keep me from believing I deserve a life-long relationship with a soulmate.

I often count my blessings, naming them one by one to remind me of God's love and how much He has done for me. I have a good job, no debt, and a small but lovely home in an idyllic community. Even though I don't always count it as a blessing, my mom lives close by in an assisted living facility. And, I have co-workers who willingly keep my identity a secret, even though they'll likely lose their jobs if they don't since I made the owner put it in my contract when he hired me.

Seriously. I should be happy. Keyword: should.

Two

Cam

I tap the Google search icon on my phone as I listen to Everly. "Moses H. Cone Memorial Park. Where is that?" I say to myself as I scroll. I click on the map, using two fingers to get a closer view.

"Looks pretty cool. How have I never been here before?" Reaching down, I pat Max on his head. "Want to check it out tomorrow, boy?" Max's heavy skull raises, making my hand bounce slightly. "Good dog. We'll make a day of it and take a lunch." Max is on his feet, drool already dripping from his wide grin. "You are too smart for your own good, Max. You've had your supper."

A gentle breeze blows across the porch carrying with it the moisture soaking the land and now the cuff of my pants. I listen as rain hits the green metal roof above me and drains into the rain barrels tucked away at the side of the cabin. The sound is as calming as Everly's voice. I strain to hear the caller's words which Everly interrupts.

"Did he just start to ask her out?" Max lays back down with a sigh. "Exactly how I feel, boy." I can't believe this guy. I don't even have enough nerve to call in just to speak with Everly. Even if I did, I have no idea what I'd say. I don't know how old she is or what she looks like. Not that it should matter, but she could be a middle-aged hag. But I surmise this isn't true, not with that voice. Smooth as room-temperature butter, it isn't quite seductive—more alluring with a professional touch. And, there is always a smile in her voice.

Max growls softly, the noise deep and low in his throat. He peers between the balusters of the deck overlooking majestic mountains. The autumn leaves are in their beginning stages of glory. Smoke rises from the cabin below me and dissipates in the now drizzling rain.

"Whatcha see, boy? Is Maggie down there?" A flit of yellow has Max on his feet, tail wagging, but he doesn't bark. Another blur of yellow catches my eye as Maggie, the neighbor's dog, bounds between trees, visible only in the small patches of green covered in a smattering of reds, oranges, and golds. Maggie barks and Max returns the call, looking to me eagerly as if seeking permission to help Maggie in her pursuit of whatever she is chasing. "Not this time Max."

The sun competes with the changing leaves as it climbs into bed in the Blue Ridge Mountains. Maggie and her bark forgotten, Max plops on his belly with a sigh. I sigh as well, neither of us seemingly content, when I should be. My job at a local commercial construction company is fulfilling, financially I have no issues, I'm healthy, yet I am not happy. I don't have the energy or inclination to be out on the town after pushing myself at work, using all my energy in business interactions. I come home completely wiped most days, so I have few friends.

Max is the recipient of most of my time and attention. Our daily runs after work clear my mind each evening, but it is the quiet of these mountains that refills my tank. I send a prayer Heavenward, thanking God for this home, even though it has come to me through profound loss.

This cabin holds fond memories of summers with my grandparents--rolling down hills, learning to shoot, sitting together at the kitchen table for homemade meals, and gathering for what Grandpa called, 'family altar.' I learned how to trust God during those summer nights.

When choosing a university, Appalachian State was at the top of my list. I begged my parents to allow me to stay in our family cabin, seldom used after my grandparents were no longer living. To Mom, I explained that if I lived off-campus, it would reduce the pull of normal college activities, and I would be able to study more. To Dad, I stated, 'It will save money.' I think this was the reason he informed Mom it was a good idea.

HEIDI GRAY MCGILL

The drizzle of rain hitting the tops of the trees below does nothing to diminish the spectacular last remnants of sunset before me. Max no longer growls but stares mesmerized, matching my own gaze and stance. Head cocked slightly, tongue sticking out, we make quite the pair. It is a bad habit and something my mother tried to correct in me as a child. Whenever I am in deep concentration, my tongue seems to need air, and the tip sneaks its way out of the right side of my mouth. In middle school, I learned to stick my pencil in its place, so it had nowhere to go. Tonight, my thoughts are on my parents rather than the song that is playing on JOY radio.

As their only child, I received everything after my parents died in a car accident. It took a year to finalize all the details involved with probate. My professors were incredible, helping me whenever needed, and I completed my coursework and Senior Capstone Experience the following year, graduating with honors. The condo in Charlotte sold quickly, given its location. I had no trouble parting with it since it held no sentimental attachment. My parents had sold our family home and moved into the up-scale condo community when I'd left for college.

Selling the beach house had been more challenging emotionally since I loved the Wilmington, NC, area. But I never once considered selling the cabin. Nestled in the trees, the front of the log cabin is not visible from the long winding driveway that snakes up the mountain. The back hovers over the expanse of trees and valley below, affording spectacular views year-round. This home and these mountains hold healing for me.

When my grandfather returned from Korea, he'd hiked these mountains until he found a spot that spoke to him. He purchased and cleared the land, notched the logs, and built a home just large enough for a single man in need of solace. My grandfather made a name for himself in the construction business. He drafted and built hundreds of homes in these mountains over the years. That was how he met my grandmother.

When he ordered 'the usual' one evening at the local diner, my grandmother's father had looked up, asked if he was from around here, and what he did for a living. By the time their meal was over, my grandfather had secured a job to repair and update a summer home the family had purchased out on the edge of town. Seeing as my grandmother was only in town for a few months, my grandfather focused all his attention on the house and the girl. Even though he was several years her senior, they'd fallen in love and were married the week before her parents returned to their home in South Carolina.

My grandfather marveled how such a fine woman could fall in love with a man like him. He always felt he'd been the winner in that relationship.

When Grandpa finally retired because he was unable to do the physical labor or the mental calculations needed, he passed his business down to my father. My dad expanded the business to Charlotte, where he eventually put down his roots. Like his father, my dad had married up. Only my mother was nothing like my grandmother.

My mother wanted to continue with the social status she enjoyed. Dad had happily obliged, joining her father's company with his. Dad didn't like people to know he'd come from the hills, as many called it, and worked hard to live a lifestyle of keeping up with the Joneses. I didn't desire that life.

It had been natural for me to follow in the family's footsteps as far as a profession, only I wasn't the outgoing, charismatic salesman my father had been, nor did I possess the artistic craftsmanship of my grandfather. As a college student, I dreamed of a nine-to-five job with time to have some fun outside of work. I didn't want to run the family business, and when I inherited it, I let my lawyers know the company was for sale. They took the highest bidder, leaving me with enough money to live comfortably if I make wise choices and earn a decent yearly wage.

The only thing I'd asked the lawyers to keep was my grandfather's land and home, both of which he had added to over the years. All I wanted was the quiet of these mountains. They call to me.

The one problem with my plan to have some fun in life is that I have no friends, no social life. My colleagues are married, and most have children of various ages, keeping them busy with their families. My church is full of activities, but the singles in my age range mainly consist of university females looking for their MRS degree. I'm not interested in marriage, but I am ready for friendship. I'm not saying I'm against marriage, but I haven't found anyone who holds my attention long enough to consider it.

"Sorry, buddy." Max looks at me, and I realize he hasn't been able to read my thoughts. "You make a great companion, but I'm ready for a little more. You know, someone who talks back to me." Everly's voice soothes me even as she speaks with a young teenager who wouldn't be allowed to date yet if she were my daughter. Here this girl is struggling between two young juveniles while I spend my Friday nights on a date with Everly on the air.

Tonight is pretty typical--Max beside me watching the sunset and me musing about the past and 'what if's' of the future. Max's snoring and the quiet noises of the night around me are what I usually listen to, but since it is Friday, I seek Everly's voice. My feet are propped up on the stool in front of the wicker furniture as I watch the last rays of light creating hues of purples and pinks on the undersides of the clouds. Rain no longer falls, and I venture from beneath the awning and peer over the railing. The trees below are now nearly covered in shadow. I can see lights flicking on in homes across the valley. Alexa continues to spread Everly's voice over the deck and my heart.

"Thank you for inviting me into your home this Friday evening. We here at JOY radio pray your weekend is full of joyous encounters. Remember to choose joy in every circumstance. Until next week, this is Everly Johnson, your Christian Singles Advice Host at WJOY radio, Blowing Rock, NC."

"Alexa. Off." Silence hits me like the rush of wind I feel coming in. Even the night sounds quiet at my harsh tone. I pick up the cushions from the chairs and store them in the container on the porch. The chairs are much in need of a fresh coat of spray paint. Maybe I'll do that tomorrow if the weather holds.

"No." Max's head pops up at the sound. "Sorry, boy. I almost made other plans. Well, let's get ourselves to bed so we can get an early start. Tomorrow we're in search of Everly." A smile creeps over my face at the thought. Maybe Max will use his charm on her. I know she likes dogs. She hasn't said what type, but I don't see her as a lap dog kind of girl. Max, however, can be intimidating.

Max's square head, stocky, muscular body, and short gray coat--sleek and shiny when the sun hits just right--gives away his breed. Just his size is enough to make most people veer away. It's evident he has Pitbull in him, invoking unnecessary fear in most. Some fear the large mouth, but I can't understand why. When Max pants, his full open mouth makes him look like the Disney character, Goofy, just with more teeth. I stand, Max immediately following. He may not be a pure breed, but he is intelligent, obedient, and an excellent companion.

I laugh, shutting the French doors behind me, repeating the words my grandfather said every night before going to bed. "Max, tomorrow is the first day of the rest of our lives."

Three

Everly

Scott is more quiet than usual in the car as he drives me home from the radio station.

"What happened today?"

He's been my best friend since my freshman and his junior year at Mount Vernon Nazarene University. He knows when I'm off.

"Mom happened. I went to see her before work. She's got another boyfriend." I draw out 'another' like a sullen teenager.

"Seriously?"

"I know, right? As if four husbands aren't enough." I turn my face to the window, not wanting Scott to see the sheen in my eyes. All my life, Mom has chosen a man over me.

"You know she loves you, Everly."

It feels so odd hearing him use my radio personality name outside of the station. It takes effort for him to keep from calling me Evie at work. Everly is my given name, but no one calls me that, not since Junior High. My mom introduced me to the secretary of my new school, not noticing that the woman was on the loudspeaker giving announcements. The entire school heard. Teachers never bothered using my given name. By the time I'd hit high school, I was using a white cane, my vision reduced to a few degrees. Everyone seemed to know who I was then—Evie, the blind girl.

Johnson, the last name I've chosen for my radio name, is ordinary enough and flows well. My birth certificate declares I am Everly Peabody, which had been my mother's maiden name. She hadn't seen fit to give me my father's last name. I'm not even sure who he is, not that it matters. He's given me two things, his green eyes, and the Retinitis Pigmentosa gene.

Few people know my real name, and Scott works hard to ensure it stays that way. He's been my protector from the first time we ran into each other, literally, on campus. I'd swung open the doors to the Communication Department classrooms and whacked him in the back of the head. He shouldn't have been standing in the way. The memory makes me giggle.

"You know I still have that knot on the back of my head. Permanent damage."

"How did you know that's what I was thinking?"

My head swivels in his direction, my voice expressing my amazement.

"I always know." His voice holds a hint of something I can't explain. "So, are you going to tell me what's really bothering you?"

"She's dying, Scott. Why would she intentionally seek out another husband." My words are a mixture of resignation and question.

"She's lonely." Quiet envelops us. "Have you met him?"

I nod. The sound of gravel under tires welcomes me home. I hear Scott shift in his seat after putting the car in park.

"Want to pray about it?"

I don't acknowledge his words. Scott knows my answer.

"Lord," he starts without hesitation, "my best friend...."

Tears begin to flow as Scott prays for me. I'm not even sure why I'm crying, but those three words 'my best friend' have turned on the faucet. So much inside of me is bottled up tight. If I don't get the tears under control, I'll cry all night.

"Amen."

I haven't heard more of what Scott has prayed, but I know I can trust whatever he's said.

"I'll carry the flowers up for you. The card is still

attached." I hear the teasing in his voice.

"Oh, for Pete's sake. Open the stupid card." It works. He's effectively stopped my tears. He grunts as he reaches into the back seat to grab the card.

"My dearest, darling."

"Seriously, Scott." My cross tone must not be convincing since he laughs, so I punch him, missing his shoulder and hitting him squarely in the chest since he's turned in his seat.

"Okay, okay. I'll read what it really says."

He clears his throat as if he is getting ready for a grand performance, but I hear the rustle of his shirt and figure he is stalling as he rubs the spot where I've hit him.

"Miss Johnson," he starts. "Thank you for encouraging me to follow my heart. She said, 'Yes!'"

"Aw, that's so sweet. It's been a while since I received thank you flowers." Warmth spreads through my middle. If the guy is thoughtful enough to send flowers to me, the girl he is marrying is one lucky gal.

"Hey, before I forget, Mom wants to know if you'll join us for church on Sunday and dinner at our house after. Says she needs some female companionship or something like that." From his tone, I guess Scott rolls his eyes.

"Sure. I'd like that. I always enjoy the preaching and music at Alliance Bible Fellowship."

"Great!" His voice cracks. "I mean, great. Mom will be pleased."

Nodding, I grab my bag and open my door.

"Oh, let me get the flowers."

He follows me then places the vase on the kitchen table. I hear him shuffling his feet, his weight moving from one foot to the other. He does that when he's nervous, and I can't imagine what's on his mind, but I am slap worn out after work. Shame on me for not asking, but I don't.

"Well, I'll see you on Sunday. I'll pick you up at 9:30." He pauses as if he has something else to say. "I'll let myself out."

"Night, Scott. Thanks again for the ride."

"Always my pleasure, Everly."

I hear the door close but remain facing it for several moments. Something feels different. I listen to the sounds of the old house, but nothing seems unusual. Placing my belongings in their usual spots, I set my phone on its charger, stick a pod of decaf in my Keurig wannabe, and head to the back of the house to pour some lavender bath salts and bubbles into the overly large, porcelain-coated, cast-iron tub.

I am sitting in the tub, nursing my coffee; guilt washes over me. Scott always has time for me, always asks about my day, is always available when I need him. I've let him down tonight. Water covers my head as I sink under the bubbles, my coffee safely above sea level.

"Hey, there, Miss Evie!" The sweet southern drawl makes the head nurse's few words sound like a much longer sentence.

"Hello, Darla. Good to see you today." I hear her chuckle before responding.

"You are always good for a laugh, Miss Evie. Let me take those flowers. Mmm, these are nice. Who sent them this time?"

"A friend."

Her laugh sounds like tinkling bells.

"You do beat all. I need you to give me some advice on how to get my man to send me flowers like this."

She has no idea what I do for a living. She knows me only as Evie, my mom's daughter. She has yet to ask my last name. When Mom took up residence here, she made it very clear she had been married four times and couldn't remember which one had been my father. The clink of glass connecting with a hard surface lets me know Darla has set the vase down.

"Who would you like me to give them to this morning?"

"Who needs them most?"

"Not your mama. That's for certain."

"Where is Mom?"

"Now, where do you think she is? She's in the game room with..." Darla's voice is getting louder with each word, so I know she is getting near. I feel her uniform graze my extended arm as she leans in, whispering conspiratorially in my ear. "...Mr. Wonderful, as she calls him." My heart drops, but I smile.

"Are they behaving themselves?" My practiced smile is coming in handy.

"Acting like two love-struck teenagers." Her voice quiets. I feel her warm breath still near my ear. "The Director had to remind them of the house rules. I think your mama was embarrassed, but Mr. Wonderful just laughed and said rules were made to be broken. Rumor is they are talking about getting married. Isn't that just the sweetest thing you ever heard?"

"Yes. The sweetest." There are days I am thankful for the sunglasses I frequently wear. My eye roll is epic, and she would be shocked if she could see my genuine response hidden behind my Aviators.

"Well, I think our newest resident at Autumn Care may appreciate those beautiful flowers. Can you make your way to the game room?"

"Yes. Thank you, Darla." My cane connects with the wall to the right, and I follow the corridor to the end of the hall. I never understood why they named this place Autumn Care. It's as if they've covered one season but left the residents on their own for the remaining three. Or maybe they only expect the residents to live for a season. In any case, it should have been called Lovers Lane for as much sparking as goes on in this place. The sound of a volunteer yelling, "B2. B as in boy and the number two," lets me know I've arrived.

"Boy? Whose boy?" one shaky but surprisingly loud voice rings out.

"The letter B as in boy," someone with a sharper tone but equally as loud a voice quickly replies.

"When I was in the Army, B was for Bravo. You know the military alphabet was used as code...."

"We know, we know. You are Echo Tango Sierra," another resident cuts off the veteran. I hold back my laugh, recognizing the euphemism for someone about to complete his tour of duty, or in this case, tour of life.

I stand in the doorway, getting my bearings, when I hear Mom's voice off to the right. Teenage schoolgirl comes to mind as I turn in the direction of the sound. I move closer, navigating around wheelchairs and who knows what else before clearing my throat.

"Hey there, Mom."

"Darling! Jack, you remember my daughter, Evie. Evie, darling, you were just here yesterday. What brings you again so soon?"

Every other person in this assisted living facility craves family visits. Not my mom. Once a week is gracious plenty for her. A feeling, as if I've inconvenienced her, weighs me down.

"Flowers. I didn't want them to wilt." My response is dry, devoid of feeling.

"Darling, you really should marry one of those men."

That term, 'darling' grates on my nerves like fingernails on a chalkboard. She may think of it as an endearment, but when it is overused and holds no meaning, it is as distasteful as the fake smile she wears when she says it. I hear a giggle followed by a half-hearted slap and wonder if Mr. Wonderful is breaking more rules.

"Jack here, he knows how to treat a lady."

"When she's as lovely as you are...."

TMI. My stomach does a little flip when I hear the loud smack of lips. Gross. Seriously? Kissing?

"Well, I just wanted to stop and say, 'Hi.'" I am being ignored, as usual. The yell of "BINGO!" makes me jump. "So good to see you, Mom. Mr...."

"Jack, call me Jack."

"Okay, Jack. Nice to see you again." It is a common phrase that holds no meaning to me. I see varying degrees of light, but I've long ago lost the ability to see shapes or colors. I turn to go, half wishing for a 'goodbye,' 'have a nice day,' anything, but the giggle and whispers at my back tell me the two lovebirds are once again engrossed in each other.

"Leaving us so soon, Miss Evie?" Darla's words hold a hint of concern. She gives and gives to her patients and still has enough left over for me.

"Yes. I just popped in to say a quick 'howdy-do.'"

"You know, I'm sure your mama is just caught up in this new man of hers."

Darla is keenly aware of how my mother treats me, so I'm not surprised at her response, but the truth still hurts. My mother has always filled her life with everything but me. I know she is embarrassed by me, my handicap.

My mother hasn't given me much in my life, but if I've learned one thing from her, it is how to fake a smile. I'm good, very good, at it.

"I'm sure you're right," I say through my smile. "Isn't it fun finding love at this stage of life?"

"What a wonderful attitude." Thankfully, Darla doesn't detect my sarcasm. A sound comes from the nurse's station. "Well, according to this light, I'm needed in room 102. I see your Uber stayed. He's right out front where you left him."

"Thanks, Darla. See you next time."

"I look forward to it, honey."

"Me, too," I call back. Darla's words are sincere; mine...not so much.

The Uber driver is one of my usuals. He opens the door for me like I'm a dignitary.

"Where to now, Evie?"

"Thanks for waiting, Nick. Drop me at Moses H. Cone, please. I think I'll take a walk today."

"You got it. Cone Manor entrance or Bass Lake entrance?"

"Lake, please."

Nick is one of the better drivers. He takes the mountain curves smoothly and doesn't try to make idle conversation. I turn my head to the window even though I can't see outside.

"Do you listen to this station?" Nick interrupts my musings.

"Hmm?"

"JOY radio. Do you listen? You were humming to the song."

"Oh. I hadn't noticed. I'm sorry." I am genuinely embarrassed. I can carry a tune, but I'm no Lauren Daigle. "And, yes. I like this station and this song."

"Do you ever listen to the Friday night dating advice girl, Everly?"

Dating advice girl...really? "Sure. Doesn't everybody?" My words come out like a half-laugh.

"She seemed a little off her game last night. Like she was distracted or something."

"Right. Yeah, I noticed that as well. Maybe she'd had a tough day." I hope my burning cheeks aren't as red as they feel.

"You know, you're right. She's human, too. It's just that she always seems to have it all together. I called her once."

"You did?" I wrack my brain to remember his voice. I usually place a voice. Nothing comes to mind.

"Sure did. I got cold feet and hung up when some guy answered. Kinda freaked me out, even though he probably screens all the calls for crazies."

"Yeah." It comes out more like a sigh than a laugh, but I hope he hasn't noticed. "I bet they get some odd calls." So much for Nick not being one for small talk. I turn my face back toward the window. He must notice because he doesn't continue.

"Well, Evie, here we are. You are in the lot nearest Bass Lake." He jumps out and opens my door for me. "I'm working all day, so I'll watch for your return trip home."

"Thanks, Nick. I'm not sure how long I'll be. I didn't bring a lunch, just a protein bar, and water, so I'll probably walk to the apple barn and back today." I hear the door shut.

"Turn thirty degrees to your right. The stairs

going down to the lake are about fifty steps away."

"Thanks, Nick." I follow his directions and adjust my body, my cane tapping left and right as my feet follow in the precise path my cane has confirmed is clear. I always appreciate how Nick doesn't treat me like an invalid. He accepts my disability and makes me feel self-sufficient, something I've been my entire life. Air whooshes out my nose as my shoulders droop. I've had to be self-sufficient.

Four

Cam

"I can't believe I've lived here this long and have never been to this place." Max shakes his head at me like I'm an idiot.

Condensation from my plastic water bottle drips from my hand, making it slippery to hold. Our lunch is long gone. Not being a hiker, I haven't adequately prepared. I've remembered doggie waste bags yet forgotten to bring anything for Max to drink out of.

"Sorry, boy. We're almost back to the lake. You'll have to get your drink from there." Guilt fills me as I gulp down the last of the water. Max gives me the stink eye as I crush the container, making it as compact as possible, before securing the lid so it will fit in my pants pocket until I find a recycle bin.

I've seen several women hiking this morning, but none I think might be Everly. Maybe I've come too early this Saturday morning, or perhaps, she is walking another of the twenty-five miles of carriage trails. Max and I set a leisurely pace and head back toward Bass Lake.

Daydreaming is a bad habit, and I realize I'm doing it when Max barks, pulling me with him when he lunges forward. My wrist burns as the leash strangles it. I have no choice but to follow.

"Max, stop!" I quickly glance to see who he is about to attack before experiencing a Marmaduke moment. Flying through the air behind the leash of my dog, realization dawns--what goes up must come down. I hear a scream before being submerged in the lake. Through a waterfall of hair, I attempt to look around to see who Max has frightened. I now recognize the cry was my own. Great. At least no one saw me.

"Max," I spit out between clenched teeth that are full of grit.

"Are you okay?"

Genuine concern fills the voice as dread fills my mind. I'm flat on my stomach, trying to blend in with the muck surrounding me. That's a little hard to do when my outstretched arm is still holding the leash of a frantically barking dog, desperately trying to reach whatever caught his attention. I can't quickly turn around, and I'm not sure I want her to see my face. I swallow, which is not a good idea.

"Good. All good," I spurt out between chokes. "Nothing a little Tide won't fix." I've surprised myself with my quip. I'm usually pretty slow doling them out, and even slower catching ones sent my way.

"So I see."

The *slurp, suck, drip* of me removing myself from sludge is followed by the *slosh, squish, squeak* of my shoes as I struggle to get up the small embankment. Max reaches the level ground before me and begins his wet dog dance. Max can throw an impressive amount of water a fair distance when performing his after-water ritual, even with short hair.

"Oh!"

I'm guessing from the surprise I hear in her voice, that Max has set a new Olympic record for distance. I can't precisely tell since brown water is running from my too-long hair into my eyes, blurring my vision. I resist the temptation to shake as well.

"I'm guessing Max is yours?"

There is a smile in her voice. Something feels familiar about it. I wipe my eyes with my free hand only to realize, too late, that bottom-of-the-lake goo covers it. Max sits beside me, grinning from ear to ear, very pleased with all that has transpired.

"Yes, Max is mine." I hold out his leash. "Would you mind holding this for a minute so I can wipe myself off?" When there is no response, I blink a few times to clear my eyes. I expect to see fear, but instead, I see a blur of blond hair bending down, arms outstretched like she is ready to catch a toddler just learning to walk.

"Come here, boy. He is a boy, right? With a name like Max...well, I suppose it could be short for Maxine."

Her arms are still outstretched. I let go of the leash, and he saunters to her, placing his big bony head in her right hand.

"Thanks. Yes, Max is a boy. A bad boy." Lifting the bottom of my shirt, I realize there is not a single spot on my clothing that is not dirty.

"If you need something to dry off with, you are welcome to this." She produces a small, bright orange microfiber cloth from her backpack.

"Thanks." I reach out and, for the first time, see her smiling face. Sunglasses cover her eyes, but I'm sure I've seen her before. "Do I know you?" Her smile quickly fades.

"I'm not sure." Her reply is curt, but I continue.

"Wait, didn't I see you at Camp Coffee Roasters yesterday?"

"Hmm..." Crouching back down, she pats Max's wet head as if contemplating the possibility. "I don't remember seeing you."

"I'm usually pretty good at remembering faces." My muffled words trail off behind the towel. Face still covered; I may leave it there. Recognition dawns; she's the blind girl I ran into because I was looking at my phone. Her joke catches up to me, and now my brown muddy face also sports a lovely shade of red. I hear her laugh as I slowly lower the towel and wonder if I missed a spot before mentally slapping myself.

"So, was the coffee for you or Max here?"

Her smile has returned, and Max has moved in for the kill, his head resting so hard on her shoulder he knocks her off balance. Before I can stop him, Max is in her lap.

"Max! Off!"

"No, he's fine. I love dogs. I just never expected one this large, or this heavy, to consider himself a lap dog." The lilt of her voice reminds me of a child experiencing true joy. "You're a good dog," she murmurs.

For a moment, as she scratches him behind the ear, I have a slight twinge of jealousy.

"Sorry about that. That's the one command he never seems to obey. Now you're covered in mud." I pull Max by the collar and give him the command to lay down. I think he raises an eyebrow before complying. The silent communication between us sends sparks flying. We'll need to have a talk when we get home. Max and I finally break eye contact. I think he wins.

"No. It's fine. No harm done. He's a cutie." She doesn't even brush herself off, just stands.

I hold out the rag, no longer orange—more like

camo for fall, before realizing she can't see me. Even so, she holds out her hand.

"Thanks," I say, handing it back only to realize her hands are now covered. "Wait, it's pretty gross." I pull back on the rag, but she has a good grip. We stand there playing tug-of-war before I let go.

"Remind me not to challenge you to an arm wrestle," she jokes.

I pick up Max's leash; he doesn't budge. "Heel." The command is familiar; he is used to being on my left and maintaining a consistent pace when I jog. It's like I can see the wheels turning in his head. He looks between me and the girl...the girl!

"Sorry, I should have introduced myself. I'm Cameron Boyd. Cam to my friends." I stick out my hand, and surprisingly she puts hers out as well. I adjust and grasp hers.

"Evie. It's a pleasure to meet you."

After the briefest pause, she loosens her grip. I'm sure she expects me to say something else, but I've maxed out my word limit and creativity at this point. I grasp for something to say, but she beats me to it.

"I'm headed up to the parking lot. Since I ventured off the path to save a damsel in distress...."

"Seriously?" Her laugh is contagious and my attempt at being incredulous falls short. "Okay. So, I scream like a girl. You would, too, if you'd been in my shoes."

"I am a girl, and I promise you, I do not scream like that." Her smile widens. "Anyway, like I was saying...I got a little turned around when body-slammed by this sweet boy."

I realize Max is not beside me but standing at a perfect heel to her left, his shoulder slightly grazing her leg. She reaches down and places her hand on his head. It's like watching butter on a hot ear of corn; he melts into her side.

"Would you mind directing me to the parking area?" Her words barely register in my mind.

"Oh, yeah. Sure. I'm headed that way myself. I'll walk with you." I'm not sure if I need to take her arm, or what. It feels awkward.

"Direction?"

"Right. I mean, not right as in turn right, but right as in...." Her laugh makes me smile. Here I am dripping who knows what small creatures into my once white running shoes, and I'm smiling. "Make a quarter turn to your left and head up the hill."

I marvel as I watch her. Her cane in her right hand moves in sync with each step. When the cane taps from her left to her right, she moves her left foot forward into the space she has just identified as clear. The process has me fascinated and mesmerized.

"Hey, man. Better hold onto your dog," some guy

on a bicycle yells as he zooms past.

I haven't even realized Max is in perfect step with Evie, his eyes alternately watching the cane and looking up to her. I notice I am doing the same. Heat floods my face, and I'm grateful she can't see it or the rest of me. She reaches down and runs her hand over his back to his neck, finds the collar, then slides it down the leash until she holds the loop. By the time we reach the steps up to the parking lot, I feel replaced and jealous. Definitely jealous.

"Is that your Jeep?" I ask her when we reach the top. Only the Jeep with a bike rack and my car are parked nearby.

"Did you really just ask me that question?"

She can't hide her amusement, and the laughter that bubbles forth has me momentarily confused. My hand slaps my forehead, sending a smattering of dirt flying. I can't figure out how to respond to my stupidity but make an attempt anyway.

"Evie, I'm…."

"Cam, I haven't laughed this hard or this many times in weeks. You seriously crack me up."

Fumbling for my keys, anything to keep from eating more dirty feet, I say the first thing that comes to mind. "So, how are you getting home?"

"Uber. I had just pulled my phone out to arrange my ride when I heard you scream…like a girl."

She is something else. I ignore the jab. "I'm happy

to give you a ride home." The words are out of my mouth before I have time to think about how they sound. It is the twenty-first century, after all. Getting into the car with someone you don't know is not smart. "I mean, Max here will guard you. Obviously, he likes you better than he likes me." I make a face at Max, and a low growl emanates from his chest. "See what I mean?"

She hesitates, but her hand never stops petting Max, who still stands by her side. "I'm not far. I'd appreciate the ride if you don't mind."

"Of course. It's the least I can do." I reach for the door handle and see dirty water still dripping from my shirt sleeve. "You can sit up front. Max, in the back," I order, giving him the same stink-eye he gave me earlier. "Max is a seat hog, so you'll have more room up front." That laugh again. What a sound. I shut the door on Max as she settles in before closing her door. I pop the trunk, surprised my fob still works, and grab a towel.

"I should have brought the truck," I say after opening my door and laying the towel across the seat, hoping to keep the fabric as clean as possible. Max places both paws on the console between the seats and smiles at me, seemingly proud of the artwork his paws have made on the back seat. Buckling up, I see Evie fiddling with her phone.

"Second thoughts about the ride?"

"Oh, no. All good." A flash of light catches me off

guard. "Just taking your picture and sending it to my family and friends so they'll know who to look for if I suddenly disappear." She laughs, but I can't tell if she's teasing or telling the truth.

Five

Everly

I'm crazy. I've lost my mind. Not only am I in the car with a stranger, but I've also just given him my home address. Anyplace else would have been wiser. My mind is a jumbled mess warring between 'what ifs' and 'no worries.' I pretend to send the picture, having no idea if he is watching. My hands are shaking nearly as hard as my stomach is quivering—the 'what ifs' are winning.

Warm air blows over my ear, and I freeze. Would this guy take advantage of me in a public parking lot? Hadn't he mentioned there were only two cars around? A scream builds and is ready to burst forth.

"Max. Lay down." A low growl reverberates in my ear, and I realize Max isn't moving even at Cam's command. "Max." Cam drags out the word, and I wonder if he'll count to three like a toddler mom.

"He's not bothering me." My shaky hand reaches up, grazing Max under the chin. Drool runs down my wrist. "He makes a good chaperone."

"Do we need one?"

Cam's voice is neither teasing nor flirtatious. He is entirely clueless, which makes me smile; my racing heart slows. The woman's voice on the overly loud Waze app voice startles me. Max growls, and I feel his muscles tense.

"It's okay, boy," I murmur.

"Sorry about that. I forgot to turn down my volume."

Cam is busy fumbling with his phone, so I take two deep breaths to help calm my nerves. Max rubs his soft ear against my cheek.

"Here we go, into the wild blue yonder..."

Cam singing those words release the last of my tension, and I laugh louder than Waze Girl, who is yelling at us to head south on Service Road toward State Road 1552.

"Let me guess; you are not former military." It's more of a statement than a question.

"What? Oh, sorry, my grandfather served. He used to sing that all the time."

I recognize the sentimental tone and immediately rein in my former thoughts. It would be easy to rib him, but it doesn't feel right.

"Is he still living?"

"No, he passed a few years ago. I inherited his

house outside of town. Do you like living so close to downtown?"

Conversation flows easily. We chat, skirting personal subjects. Thankfully he hasn't asked me what I do for a living. Waze Girl announces we've arrived at our destination, and I'm not particularly pleased with her.

"Cute house. 1930's?"

"Yes. How did you know?" I'm surprised.

"Low pitched gable roof, wide-overhanging eaves, ample front porch." His voice trails off, a tinge of embarrassment in his tone.

"How does that place it in that time frame?" My question is genuine, but he seems taken back by the fact that I'm acting interested, which I am.

"Well," he pauses, "you really want to know?"

Now I'm sure he knows the answer; he just isn't sure if I genuinely want to hear it. "Of course." I turn in my seat to face him to emphasize my point even though I can't see him.

"Your home is made of natural materials. Clapboard siding, to be exact."

I can tell he is looking out the front window and occasionally turning to face me. I nod to let him know I'm listening.

"You've kept the integrity of the home even though HardiPlank® would have been a better insulator and still looked similar, which brings me to the windows. Those are originals and need caulking."

"I'll keep that in mind. Thank you."

"Sears, Roebuck & Company, and other companies sold this style home from catalogs."

"You can tell all of that by looking out a car window?"

"Sure."

"But couldn't it have been built any time between a certain number of years? How can you be so sure it was 1930?"

"Well, the historic marker on the porch is a pretty good indicator."

He is smiling. I don't have to have my vision to catch that.

"Cam, you're a hoot." I shift my body and feel for the door handle. He is out of his seat and opening my door before I have located it.

"Thanks for coming to my rescue today."

His words are quiet, not like it is hard for him to say them, more...I'm not sure.

"Thank you for the ride. It's been nice talking with you and meeting Max." Max barks as if he understands what I'm saying. "Bye, Max." I open my cane and head toward my front porch. The car door shuts behind me, but no footsteps follow. "Bye, Cam. See you around."

Inside I follow my familiar routine of putting each item in its proper place. Slobber still covers my hand and wrist, but I don't care. Pushing my sunglasses to the top of my head, I get a whiff of wet dog. Okay, maybe I do care a little.

I place cut vegetables over my torn romaine and open a can of chickpeas as I talk with Ginger over speakerphone. We've been discussing Cam for the last ten minutes.

"He was nice." My words sound strange in my ear.

"Wait. Nice as in nice? Or more like nice nice?"

Ginger has been my friend since Junior High. I know I can't pull any wool over her eyes.

"More like…," my hesitation is too long.

"Do I need to drive up there tomorrow? Seriously, I need more details."

"Your visit is going to have to wait. Scott invited me to go with him to church on Sunday and then to his parents' house for lunch." The silence that follows disturbs me. "Ginger?"

"You know he likes you, right?"

"What? Scott? No, he's just a friend." But even as I say the words, my stomach begins to roll.

"He's liked you from the moment you tried to take him out with the door." She tries to have a light tone, but I can tell she has more to say and isn't trying to start a girlfriend 'remember when' party.

"Ginger," my breath catches in my throat, "I, I don't like him that way. Are you sure?"

"Are you sure?"

Her emphasis on 'you' makes me pause. Am I sure? He has been my constant friend. His dad owns the radio station where Scott helped me get my job. Memories flash in my mind of Scott driving my U-Haul from college to Blowing Rock, and unpacking it, so Ginger and I could take the scenic drive.

"Wow." Suddenly, the floor no longer feels solid, my legs give way, and I plop into the kitchen chair. "You're right."

"About which part?"

"He likes me. How did I not see this? Oh, Ginger, what am I going to do?"

"Well, I guess that depends on how you feel about him. I always thought you guys made a great couple." Silence. "So…do you like him? I mean, could you like him?"

How does someone answer that with this new revelation? If Scott honestly does care for me, we could have a good relationship. He is a Christian, kind, accepts me as I am, knows my background, and has never made me feel he is ashamed or embarrassed by me. He's my best friend. But is that all I will ever get out of life? I've never had a romantic feeling toward Scott. He's always been more like a brother.

"Evie?" Ginger has given me time to pull my thoughts together.

"I don't like him, Ginger. Not like that." This time the silence is on her end of the line. "Wait. Ginger, do you like him?" Still silence. "Why didn't you ever tell me? Seriously! How long have you liked him?"

"Since the day you came back from class and told me about the goofy guy you hit with the door. He treated my best friend the same way I always have and, well, the rest is history."

We continue the game of silence until I hear a faint giggle.

"What? You have a plan. I know it. Spill the beans. I'm all in." Like every other ridiculous idea she's ever come up with, I agree before even hearing it.

"It's going to be epic!"

Six

Cam

"She called me Cam." Max lets out a low moan and shakes his head before plopping unceremoniously onto the back seat. I'm sure I have a goofy look on my face. But I don't care.

I'm standing in her driveway, looking up at her cute house, taking in the view of the trees surrounding her porch. On the top right, a branch has fallen and bent her gutter near the downspout.

"I should fix that for her." My words sound foreign to me. Since when do I offer to do work, especially physical labor that requires a ladder? I hear my dad's voice in my mind 'You're management now, son. Leave that work for those beneath your station.'

Yet a flicker of excitement at getting my hands dirty—not Bass Lake dirty, but handyman dirty, ignites a spark. The feeling is blotted out by the jealousy that comes over me as I consider Evie may have someone in her life who does those things for her. I never asked if she has a boyfriend. I didn't notice a ring, but then, I wasn't looking. It dawns on me she may be listening to see if I leave. I don't want to come across as creepy.

Getting in the car, I gag. "Seriously, Max. You smell like a wet dog." I laugh at my joke. My Saturday afternoon will consist of water and soap—for Max, me, and my car. I may even splurge on a bone for Max. I have him to thank for this morning's encounter.

Sunday morning dawns bright and clear. No rain today. I gauge my time and take Max for a walk to the bottom of the driveway and back up. It's just enough to get my heart pumping. In all honesty, my heart has been pumping all night long. I've Marmaduke'd into Bass Lake a dozen times in my dreams, and each time a fair-haired fairy has rescued me.

"I'll take you for a run this evening, Max. For now, I've got to get ready for church." Max smiles at me, and I reach down to take off his leash so he can do the usual and run the rest of the way to the house. Only he doesn't. Max slowly cocks his head, ears swiveling, and before I can give a command, he's off.

It's not safe in these mountains. Coyotes are an issue, but man is worse. I sit, knowing it is no use trying to track him, and I offer up a silent prayer even as I listen for a gunshot. I close my eyes, and rather than Max, Evie comes to mind immediately. I wonder what color her eyes are, the ones behind the classic Aviators? Her petite frame and blond hair make me guess blue. I replay our short time together in my mind. I feel like I've missed something and hit rewind only to show the same reel. We have probably crossed paths in town over the years, but I don't remember seeing her.

An hour later, Max saunters up on the porch stinky from whatever he's rolled in and is amazingly content. All thoughts of Evie are pushed aside. It will be another soap and water day when I return from church. Max laps up the last of the water in his bowl, and I refill it, giving him a bone to keep him busy.

"I missed the first service, Max." Water drips out of the corner of his mouth. His tongue is hanging out, and it lifts in what I'm certain is a smirk. "You do beat all, Max. If I didn't know better, I'd think you planned this." Grabbing my keys and phone from the table, I head out for the second service, locking him on the back deck so he can enjoy the beautiful day.

I see her the moment I sit down. Her folded cane peeks out of a small leather backpack, the wrist strap flopping like the loose curls of her hair as she moves. Her right hand rests on the forearm of a guy around her age. I can't hear what he is saying, but the older couple they are talking with seems delighted to see her. The woman hugs her, which Evie returns, before the older woman's eyes widen and sparkle at the young man.

"Evie." The whisper of her name on my lips burns like hot liquid and flows down to my gut, causing physical pain. I cannot tear my eyes away from the scene. Gently touching the small of her back with his left hand, the man uses his right to take hers and direct it towards the gray-haired gentleman. The motion looks natural. If I hadn't been paying close attention, I might not have noticed his giving her assistance. It seems like they know each other well. Too well.

My eyes are magnets, unable to pull away from this unseen force. Evie places her hand on his arm in a familiar way, and he leads them to their seats. The music begins, but I do not hear the words meant to give praise to my King. If I turn my head, I can see them. My neck aches, and I pull against it, keeping my focus on the stage in front of me. When we sit, I only see the hands in her lap. Hands that played tug-of-war with her towel, hands that caressed Max's head.

I hear the rustling of pages and taps on phones as congregants find the scripture. Since I have not been paying attention, I read it from the screen.

"Can a mother forget the baby at her breast and have no compassion on the child she has borne? Though she may forget, I will not forget you!" Isaiah 49:15

The scripture makes me think of my mom. Losing her was hard, but I am mostly able to remember the good things now. I smile, thinking of how opening my lunchbox to a smiley face on a sticky note was like finding pirate treasure--until middle school. I still loved discovering them but hid them like contraband from my lunch buddies and the cute little freckle-faced girl who always sat beside me. My mind drifts to Evie, and I work to bring my focus back to the pastor.

"Not everyone has an image of a mother who soothed and comforted them as a child. Our physical mothers will never measure up to the love of our Heavenly Father. We have in our imagination a view that a devoted mother – one that in all things only does what is good and beneficial for her child – is how parenting should look." I'm not sure where he is going with this, so I listen more closely.

"The problem is that every mother is flawed. Your mother may have birthed you, but God formed you." Something draws me to Evie, and I immediately look to where she is sitting. Her hands fidget. I ponder if she's wondering if God made a mistake with her. The older woman hands her a tissue, and it disappears as Evie lifts her hands then lowers them now holding a crinkled mascara-smeared tissue.

I make a decision, a bold one. I'll talk to her after church. Only, as soon as those words cross my mind, everything else goes blank. Maybe I'll just stand near the door and casually say 'hi' when they pass. That might work. The strains of a guitar and electric piano let me know I've missed the rest of the sermon. I stand with the others and sing a familiar chorus, one that doesn't require me to read the words on the screen. I mentally plan my exit to get to the door before they do.

The elderly couple beside me is taking their time. The woman returns each tissue to its proper place. I hear her mumble something about a stick of gum she knows is in there somewhere.

"Sweetheart, this young man is probably late for Sunday lunch. Let's let him get home to his family."

I smile, but the sad reality that I have no one to go home to hits me hard. My stomach grumbles as if emphasizing the man's comment.

"Oh, dear. I'm so sorry." Hastily she shoves a few items back into the abyss and takes her husband's outstretched hand.

"It's fine, really," my smile is genuine, and I pray they don't see my foot tapping out its anxiousness.

Once free, I bolt for the door, my eyes scan the crowd, but I do not see Evie. Like a child, I stand on tiptoe, peering over the heads of those around me in search of her golden hair. Nothing. Dejected, I shove my hands as deep into my skinny jeans as they will go and stay in the queue of those leaving the worship center.

Several young ladies giggle as I pass them on the sidewalk outside. I offer them a smile then inwardly groan. You'd think I'd proposed. I hear one whisper my name and wonder how she may know me. The crowd thins as families get tired toddlers and unruly preteens into vehicles. Then I hear her voice. Not Evie's, but Everly's. My heart feels like I have cheated on my one true love, only I don't know which one she is.

I search, but the voice is gone. A young mom's measured words are the only female sounds near me that I can detect. The slightly formal yet personal tone of Everly Johnson floods my mind, filling it to overflowing with confusion and doubt. For years I've listened to Everly, dreamed of what I would say if I met her, created crazy scenarios where we meet face to face and have a conversation that leads to, what, I'm not sure, but I always wake wanting more.

Now I have the opportunity, and although I am still looking long after the voice is gone, I find myself wishing more for Evie. Conversation flows easily with her. I never am at a loss for words, which is not normal for me. With my phone in my hand, I think of her snapping that ridiculous picture, and I smile.

Two vehicles away, I see the guy Evie was with shutting the passenger side door of his SUV before getting in himself. I play Frogger and cross the parking lot to my truck, dodging left to right between parked and moving cars. One wrong move, and game over.

I'm in my car and keep an eye on his vehicle. He hasn't yet pulled out. Following won't be difficult. He drives a black Toyota 4Runner with a WJOY Radio sticker on the back left window. The sticker tells me he has good taste in music. The type of vehicle reveals he either has money or likes to act as if he does. I see the older couple wave to him from their Mercedes as they pass his still parked vehicle. I hear the woman call out, 'See you at home, dear' through her open window. I amend my statement. He likely comes from money.

I back out too quickly and receive a sharp honk and profanity for my carelessness. "You'd never know this is a church parking lot," I murmur to myself as I mouth 'Sorry' and give the obligatory wave to right all wrongs. Now five vehicles ahead, I see the 4Runner turn left just before the light turns yellow. Impatience has me gripping the steering wheel, knuckles turning white. My eyes dart from the traffic light to the street to my left as the last glimpse of black fades from view.

Seven

Everly

Tears stream down my face. The pastor has reached into my chest, grabbed hold of my heart, and twisted it until I can't breathe. I feel Mrs. Hassen press a tissue into my shaking hands. So many things cloud my mind, and I can't begin to unravel my thoughts. I want to stand up and run out but know I will cause a scene, so I sit, head bowed.

I can feel Scott's leg bouncing next to mine. He isn't touching me, but I can feel the warmth of his nearness. I long to go back to when I could tell him anything, but now that I know the truth, that he cares for me, it will never be the same. This time, I'll have to work it out on my own.

He reaches over and gently places his hand under my elbow, like some Victorian gesture. I cringe, and he draws back. Everyone around me is standing. I've missed the cue that we are singing the final chorus and he has only tried to be thoughtful. I decide to remain seated. The sermon has wrecked me, and I'm spent.

"Are you okay, dear?" Mrs. Hassen lightly touches my shoulder when the service has ended.

"Oh, yes, ma'am. It was such a touching sermon. I just needed a moment." I haven't lied.

"It's Lila, dear. Please call me Lila." Her tone holds too much hope, too much excitement for a future that will never be.

"Thank you, Lila."

"Scott, dear, we'll meet you and your sweet girl at home." Lila's words confirm my suspicions.

"We have a quick errand to run, Mom. We'll be there shortly."

Scott's elbow touches my sleeve, and I reach up instinctively, taking his arm. He deftly maneuvers me through the crowd, occasionally greeting someone he knows.

"Scott,…" I start when he opens the door to his SUV.

"Not here."

Fresh tears flow. He knows. My heart aches, knowing his hurts. I say a quick prayer for words to help me let him down gently.

He pulls onto Highway 105 and doesn't go far before getting off. I feel the rough ground beneath his tires, along with a distinct rise in elevation, and know we are about to shift into 4-wheel drive. A few minutes later, he slows, rolls down the windows, and turns off the engine. I hear him turn in his seat. He doesn't say a word, allowing me to speak first. His finger pushes my hair behind my ear, the motion so gentle I barely feel his touch. I turn to him.

"Scott." His name catches in my throat. Before I can go on, Scott takes back the conversation.

"I love you. I've loved you from the first time you knocked some sense into this dull head of mine." I hear him settle back into his seat. "I'd hoped that one day you'd see me as more than just a friend."

He is quiet, and I wonder if he is crying.

"Scott. I love you, too, I just…." I struggle to get the words out and repeat my petition of the Lord to help me.

"I know. It's okay. What changed, Evie?" His voice changes to genuine confusion.

"I…" stammering, I search for words.

"Did you meet someone?"

His question catches me off guard. Did I? Is that what this is? Has Cam opened my eyes to the possibility of someone else other than Scott caring for me? What if Cam, this guy I've met once, well, technically twice, was just being nice? Even so, he did treat me kindly. It doesn't mean he has romantic notions toward me.

"I see," he says when I don't answer because my mind is a whirlwind of thoughts full of debris.

"No, I mean." I take a deep breath. "Scott, I had no idea you liked me more than friends. I guess I knew; I just didn't want our friendship to end, so I didn't accept it. Does that make sense?"

I hear him clear his throat before taking a deep breath. He bared his soul to me, and I am making a mess of things.

"Your mom expects us to get married, doesn't she?" My words come out quiet, resigned.

"Yes. Mom's been after me for years."

Now I'm the one turning in my seat. "Years?"

"Yes, years." Scott's chuckle at my surprise makes me smile.

"I'm such a dolt. How did I not know?"

"Maybe you missed all the visible cues."

Now we both laugh. I try to punch him, but he is faster this time, and my fist connects with the seat-back. We're quiet for a few moments.

"Scott, are you okay? I mean, I'm so sorry." A piece of my heart is breaking off.

"I will be. Now, let's head to Mom and Dad's for pot roast, then play a game. Maybe hide-and-go-seek. You can be 'it.'"

I hear the car start and know where his arm is now. This time I don't miss it.

The good thing about my schedule is I only work Wednesday through Friday evenings. The bad thing about my schedule is I only work Wednesday through Friday evenings. That means filling the other days of the week can be challenging.

My eyes open Monday morning to the chirping of birds, but I do not feel their joy. Sunday dinner had not only been awkward, but the ordinarily light-hearted banter with Scott felt stilted. I apologized, letting Lila know I had a headache, and Scott took me home right after dessert.

I lay under my IKEA goose-down duvet and re-play every moment in my mind.

The ride home is quiet. When Scott walks me to my front door, he pauses, and I remember him doing the same the last time he brought me home. How could I have missed so many signals?

His hands lightly touch my shoulders, slowly moving up my neck. A slow panic starts, and I can't decide if I want him to kiss me to see if there is any spark at all or if I don't want to know. I feel his lips softly caress the top of my forehead before his connects with mine. His breath is like my own, unsteady.

"We'll always be best of friends, right, Princess?"

I'm sure he means well calling me that. He's never called me that before and it feels awkward and forced, as if he wishes he could call me something more.

"I don't want to lose you." There is genuine concern in his voice.

My arms wrap around him with a fierceness I do not know I possess. Every ounce of me tries to meld into him, letting him know we are as one, even as I know we will never be. At least not as God intended.

"Yes." I feel my words vibrate against his chest as he hugs me back with the same intensity.

We stand there until I realize I am crying. His shirt is damp when he pulls me away. His thumb caresses my cheek, and I lean into the touch. I do love him, but I'm not in love with him. My hand covers his as it cradles my cheek. I kiss his palm before letting go. It is the most intimate we have ever been, and I will cherish it always.

I place my warm hands on my damp cheeks. There is no going back, no changing my mind. I should call Ginger, but my wounded heart needs time. And, I still need to work through the issue with my mom in light of Sunday's sermon.

As if she read my mind, my phone dings with Ginger's familiar text ringtone.

(Sent from iPhone)

> **Ginger:** I'm driving down this weekend. Don't tell me no.

> **Ginger:** I'll pick you up from work on Friday evening.

I laugh. How am I so blessed and cursed to have two best friends who know me better than I know myself?

(Sent from iPhone)

> **Everly:** RSVP'ing NO to the ball at the castle just for you. Who needs a Prince, anyway?

I am about to say 'send' then tell my phone to delete, and I dictate a different text.

(Sent from iPhone)

> **Everly:** You're the best. I talked with Scott. I'll share deets over pizza on Friday. You're buying.

I send this one.

I'm too raw to mull over the mom issue, so head outside to rake leaves. The sun is shining, and the warmth feels like God smiling down on me. The words from the sermon won't let me go, 'Your mother may have birthed you, but God formed you.' I let them ruminate as I gather what I need to rake the newly fallen leaves.

My postage stamp front yard doesn't take a lot of

work, and, although not perfectly done, it feels good to rake the leaves and stuff them into brown paper bags. I'm on my second bag when I hear a large, older vehicle, or poorly maintained new one, pull into my gravel driveway.

"Hey."

It's all I get to determine the identity of my visitor.

"Hey," I reply, hoping for more clues.

"Need some help?"

I'm about to say 'no thanks' to this kind stranger when the voice comes to me.

"Cam?"

"I took the day off. I thought I'd see if I could help some elderly folk with chores or something."

I hear the teasing in his voice and don't bite. "Oh, yes, well, Mrs. Phillips next door needs her rhododendrons trimmed back." I have no idea if this is the season to do such a thing or if Mrs. Phillips even has a bush. His laugh reaches out to me.

"Actually," he draws out the word, "Max needs to pee and asked if he could use your yard."

To this I burst out laughing. My knees buckle and my backside lands square in the middle of my recently raked stack. Without warning, Max body-slams me. Before I can catch my breath, all four paws secure me to the ground.

"Hey there, Max. Miss me?"

"He did. I tried to tell him it would seem like stalking if we came by, but...."

I recognize Cam's nervousness through the shifting of his feet on gravel. So similar to Scott. My mind begins to wonder if it is for the same reasons.

"Are you going to come up here and get your dog off of me or leave me like this?"

"I don't know. It depends on what's for lunch."

The nearly girlish giggle he adds at the end tells me this is not his typical banter, making me smile. He feels comfortable with me.

"Hot dogs for Max here," I rub his belly, which is accessible from my current position. "Chopped liver for you." Footsteps come closer.

"Max, sit."

"Oomph." Max obeys too well and sits down on my abdomen, knocking the last of the air out of me.

"Sorry!"

I feel Max reluctantly being pulled from my body, but I don't move, not that I can. I'm thankful for the leaves under me until I finally sit up and find them entangled in my hair. The giggle returns, only this time it isn't from nervousness. He's laughing at me. It sounds wonderful, but I hide my true feelings and adopt a haughty tone.

"Do you always laugh at damsels in distress?"

"You laughed at me."

He realizes he's incriminated himself and we chuckle at the same time.

"How about a cup of coffee?" I reach my hand up, and he quickly takes it as if he had been waiting for permission to do so. Electricity shoots up my arm, and I wonder if I'm hurt. But when he releases my hand, the jolt is gone.

Cam picks two leaves from my hair, then brushes off my back, stopping just above my jeans. I reach around and finish for him. I hear him clear his throat and guess he is a gentleman.

Unlike Scott, who hates coffee, Cam likes his black, and we enjoy small talk while I brew a large pot and Max curls up on the foam mat in front of my kitchen sink. I'm not sure why I'm comparing Cam and Scott and tell myself to stop.

"I think he likes you…your house," Cam quickly corrects himself as I set a mug of coffee in front of him. "Thanks." I hear his contented sigh after his first sip. Scott has never understood my coffee craze. "Good coffee."

"Why the day off?" I must catch him off guard with my question because he chokes. I stand and get two napkins, placing one within his reach.

"We've had so much rain lately, and I needed a day."

"Do you like your work?" I was moving into territory best left alone, yet I press on.

"I do. I got my degree in Building Sciences at App state. I worked grunt jobs for my dad every summer since I was fifteen and knew construction was for me. Only now, I spend more time identifying problems and coordinating crews to do the work. I miss the labor. Actually, when I was here last, I noticed you have a gutter that needs repairing. I've got some tools in the truck if you'd like for me to take a look."

"Can I afford you?" My smile is wide.

"Me, yes. Max, he charges double for anything that doesn't include ice cream for dessert."

I laugh and hear Max snort. "Whew!" I fake exasperation and wipe my hand across my forehead only to realize I am not wearing my sunglasses. Cam hasn't seemed phased.

Unlike individuals who have lost their sight due to accidents or have been blind since birth, my eyes can still track and turn in the direction of sound. This makes some people uncomfortable. Ginger's classic line is 'Look up. You're worse than a guy. My eyes are up a bit higher.'

"Your eyes are a lovely shade of green. More gray than emerald. I would have guessed blue." His words are breathy.

"My father, he,…" tears fall without warning. I've bottled my emotions for too long. With Sunday's sermon still fresh on my mind, there is no putting the cork back in now. I hear Cam stand and pour another cup. The steady stream of liquid calms me, and I take several cleansing breaths. I'm mostly back together by the time he sits down.

"I have an idea. You take care of Max and prepare lunch while I get your gutter fixed. Then let's have a picnic at Moses H. Cone."

It isn't a question, but it certainly isn't a command. It's a gift—an offering of friendship. I nod, tears starting again.

We sit in silence, listening to Max snoring. It is comfortable. This man I know little about has found a place in my heart I didn't realize needed filling. Whether or not my tears bother him, he doesn't show it. He doesn't fidget or tap his feet. He sits relaxed, enjoying his coffee.

When he heads outside, I drop to my knees on the floor and place my wet cheeks on Max's soft fur. Like Max, I curl up in a ball. He just lays there and lets me use him as a pillow. When my tears stop, I pet his head and stand. As I make chicken salad, I consider how much of my life I should share with Cam.

Max gently takes the chicken skin I offer to him, licking my fingers clean after he chews once then swallows. As I wash my hands and seal the container, I hear Cam descending the metal ladder then hear his footsteps on the porch.

"All done. I had just enough brackets to rehang the gutter." Cam launches into detailed steps of what he's accomplished. I imagine his face glowing by the sound of his voice. It's clear he loves working with his hands. "So, you shouldn't have any more issues. I would see if you could get that one tree trimmed up. A good arborist will know what to do."

"I've got a yard guy who comes once a month. I'll ask him if he knows of someone. Thanks." I pat the backpack filled with food. "Lunch is ready, are you?"

"Let me wash my hands, and I will be."

Just the comfort level of him washing his hands in my sink amazes me. It's like we've been friends for years. I hear him tear off a paper towel.

"Trash?"

"Under the sink." I hear him open the left door then the right, but I don't hear him pull out the sliding trash can.

"Evie, you've got water under here." I hear him kneel. "Hand me another paper towel."

I'm not sure of his exact location now that he's on the floor, so I slide my feet to keep from stepping on him.

"Ow." The word comes out kind of singsong and makes me laugh enough that my 'Sorry' doesn't sound genuine.

"No worries, just a knee cap. I've got two."

I hand him the paper towel and bend over as if I am also peering into the same small space.

"Turn on the water, will you?"

I turn it on and hear him feeling around.

"Now the garbage disposal." The whir of the disposal makes Max jump. "Okay, off."

"Is it serious?" My question is genuine. Working only part-time matches my disability check, but it still isn't enough to cover anything significant. I'm still wondering how much the brackets for the gutters are going to cost me. I pull my fingernail out of my mouth, knowing it gives away my nervousness. The damp paper towels hit the plastic grape bag at the top of the trash can with a *thwop* before Cam shuts the doors.

"My guess is it just needs new plumbing tape. Just don't use your garbage disposal until it's fixed. How about we enjoy the rest of the day and deal with it later this afternoon?"

"How much is this going to cost me?"

"That depends on my assistant, Max, here. He sets the number of toppings required."

It takes me a few moments to realize he is talking about pizza.

"Deal." I stick out my hand, and he takes it in his. This time the electricity feels like a hot cup of coffee on a winter day, and I don't want to let go.

Eight

Cam

I don't recognize myself, and it's a little scary. All morning I've enjoyed friendly banter and given as much as I've received, something I've never been able to do. My comfort level in Evie's home is reminiscent of summer days with my grandparents.

Stress seems to drain from me as we hike. Evie is self-sufficient, although I point out a few things that I think she might miss as we walk. I can't figure out how she knows when to get off the Lake loop, but I follow her lead. Max has made it clear he is to stay between us.

"How do you get around so well? Like, how did you know to turn off onto this path?"

"I may not see, but I can still observe."

I don't understand what she means and remain quiet.

"Sherlock Holmes reference." She changes the subject. "You seem to genuinely enjoy the hands-on part of construction, so why are you in management?"

Light glints off her Aviators. Her question is fair, and I choose the short answer.

"My dad felt it was important for me to learn from the ground up, but after I got my degree, he said it was beneath me. Large rock to your left at eleven o'clock. He wanted me to take over the family business."

"Thanks. Do you believe that? That manual labor is beneath you?"

"No, I guess not, but I enjoy what I do well enough, and the pay is decent. I've got a four-year degree, so I feel like I should use it. Besides, most construction companies can't match my salary. And the hours, especially in the summer, can be long. Bicyclist coming up behind us on your left," I mention without breaking the flow of conversation.

"Thanks. Have you ever thought of owning your own business?"

I don't answer her right away, and she seems to be giving me time to formulate my answer. My thoughts wander to summers helping my grandfather, carrying tools, feeling important. Even though I'm daydreaming, I'm aware we've turned right since Max keeps bumping his shoulder into my leg.

Whack. "Ouch."

"Tree in the face," I say it with the same emotion I have been using all day, only I'm too late this time. I stop and turn to see Evie's hand on her forehead. I pull it away. "No blood. You'll live." Her face has this incredulous look before she bursts into the loudest laugh I've ever heard, followed by a snort to rival Max's snore.

I have no idea how long we stand there. She is clutching her stomach, and I'm bent over with my hands on my knees. Max sits and stares.

"Cam, you do beat all. We have our first inside joke."

My heart flutters at Evie's words. I've never had an inside joke with a girl before. It feels good.

"You realize I'm going to look like the inept guide I am if you tell people I let you walk into a tree." I know it's true, but I find I don't mind the thought.

"Technically, the tree limb ran into me. It shouldn't have been out so far in the path." She taps her cane and begins moving again.

"Did you have a specific place in mind for us to eat? I see a clearing a ways off the path if you're willing to trust me to lead you...." Before I've finished speaking, she's closed her cane and stuck it in her pack.

"Lead on, Cameron Boyd. My life is in your hands."

She reaches for my arm, and I meet her halfway.

The warmth makes my lightweight jacket feel like goose down.

"I can't decide if you're crazy or overly trusting." I hand Max's leash to her and use my free hand to push up a low-lying apple tree limb. "Bend halfway for ten paces." She follows my instructions and stands when we are on the other side. We step over fallen logs, maneuver around holes, and skirt tangles of brambles, all with relative ease.

"Here we are." I relinquish her arm, pull out the blanket from the backpack with the food she asked me to carry, and spread it on the ground. "Left corner, two steps ahead." She takes the two steps then bends down. Max follows her every move and finds a comfortable place beside her, which, unfortunately, leaves me on the far side. Max's contented sigh lets me know he isn't moving.

"Hey, we should probably exchange numbers in case…" I can't think of a good reason. I just want her number.

"Yeah, sure."

She blurts hers out to me but doesn't pull out her phone. I quickly add it to my contacts.

"Do you want to eat now?" Her words are thoughtful.

"I didn't eat breakfast, so…." Her smile warms me. Chicken salad, Pringles, apples, and Little Debbie

Oatmeal Pies are our feast. "Do you mind if I pray?"

Her smile becomes more prominent, and she extends her hand, which I quickly take.

"Lord, thank you for this food, for the opportunity to be together with You in nature, and for my new friend. Amen." When I look up, Evie's bowed head surprises me. She doesn't release my hand for several moments. She squeezes it lightly before letting go and opening her eyes. I wonder if she has prayed silently.

"Are you a Christ Follower, Evie?" My question is bold. She turns toward me. Her sunglasses now perched on her head. I see her gray-green eyes sparkling in the sun.

"I am, and I love your word choice. It's too easy to claim to be a Christian these days. Anyone who attends church on Easter and Christmas seems to adopt that distinction. What about you?"

"I am. I accepted Jesus as my Savior when I was nine. My grandfather prayed with me one summer evening during family altar time." I glance her way, and she is slowly chewing but giving me her full attention. "Family altar was my favorite time of the day. Just before the sun went down, Grandpa, Grandma, and I would kneel in front of our chairs in the living room and talk to God. I always prayed first and would ask God to bless Mom and Dad —you know, the usual kid prayer. Then Grandma would pray for every person she knew by name.

I learned who had rheumatism, wayward children, and drinking husbands."

She chokes on a chip and takes a drink from her water bottle.

"When Grandpa prayed, it was as if God were sitting there with us. I peeked a few times just to check." She laughs. "This one night, he was silent except for the 'yes, Lord' he muttered over and over. When he finally started praying, it wasn't in his booming voice but an almost whisper. He told God all about me, how I was a good boy but one who needed God. I was crying by the time he'd finished praying. I told Grandpa I wanted to be everything he said I was, but I knew I wasn't. He smiled at me and told me how God can use people who are willing to admit they don't measure up. I prayed that night, told God every bad thing I had ever done, and asked Him to forgive me. I'll never forget that feeling."

Evie has finished her sandwich, and despite the fact I am hungry, I haven't touched mine. Memories fill me, satisfying me deep in my soul. I look over the valley below us and marvel that the God who made all of this, loved me enough to die for my sins. Max gets up and moves closer to Evie. He places his head in her lap. I follow the movement and realize she is silently crying.

She leans into Max, bending at the waist until she buries her face in his fur. I've never seen him like this and, once again, feel a pang of jealousy. When she starts to sniffle, I hand her a napkin.

"Thanks." She blows her nose, which echoes across the valley. Max is impressed. His ears go up as he follows the sound. "I haven't cried this much since, well, I just haven't cried this much, period."

"Want to talk about it?"

She turns to me. Her red-rimmed eyes aren't looking directly at me, yet, even so, they are beautiful and bore a hole into my soul.

"If you are willing to listen, I'd like to, but it may be jumbled. Scott sometimes tells me, 'Just land the plane, Evie, you'll run out of gas if you keep circling the airport.'"

"Scott?"

"My best friend and co-worker." She sighs and drops her eyes to her lap. "But that's a story for another day. Are you sure you want to hear this?"

"Yes." Plain and simple, I'd listen to her tell me how mold grows.

"Where to start. I guess I'll share my heart-change story first. I was fifteen and angry. My mother got engaged and set her wedding date for July 15th--my sixteenth birthday. Her words were, 'Who would you invite anyway, Evie? It's not like anyone would come.'"

She must have heard me gasp.

"Yeah, nice, right? I was furious and determined I

would not attend this wedding. My girlfriend Ginger had invited me to her church's summer camp, but I'd refused, using my birthday as my excuse. So, when I saw her the next day, I asked for an application. I paid for it with my babysitting money. My mom signed the form without asking a single question."

I watch as Evie picks at the grass just off the edge of the blanket before turning back my way to continue.

"The theme of the week was Lordship of one's life and how we needed to learn that dependence is better than independence from the Lord." She takes a sip from her water bottle as I finish my last bite of the sandwich. "Dependence was foreign to me. My mother had ignored me from the moment I could walk. I learned to pack my school lunch, make my meals when she was away, do laundry, stuff like that, way before any of my peers. Then when my sight got worse, I embraced independence. I didn't want anyone helping me. I was going to do it on my own. But that all changed at camp. I decided to let Christ be my guide, and I've never looked back."

I tear open a Little Debbie and pass it to her before opening my own. We sit quietly. I can tell she isn't finished, and I give her space.

"Cam, do you have a sister?"

"A sister? No. Why?"

"You're an excellent listener." She pops the last bite into her mouth and squishes the white filling out between the small gap between her front teeth.

"That is disgusting!" I laugh.

"I know, right?"

She stretches out her legs and lies down, her head on Max. I lean back but turn to face her, not wanting her out of my line of sight.

"My mom," I watch her take a deep breath and let it out slowly. "My mom is dying. She has breast cancer and has refused treatment. It has moved to other parts of her body, making it difficult for her to take care of herself all the time. She lives at Autumn Care Assisted Living." She lifts her hand, and I know not to speak. "I'm not close to my mom, but she's still my mom. At church on Sunday, the pastor reminded me that my mom isn't perfect. She may have birthed me, but God formed me. There is so much in that statement. If I accept that as truth, I need to forgive my mom for, well, everything. I also need to accept that God made me the way I am for a reason."

We are both silent for several minutes. Telling her I was in the same church service is probably not a good idea, so I let it slide, yet I mull over the consequences of not telling her. In the distance, I hear what I am sure is the clopping of horse's hooves.

"Are there horses here?" I sit up and try to peer through the trees. Evie wipes her eyes before sitting up as well.

"Do you ride?"

"I haven't. I'm a little intimidated."

The sound that comes out of her mouth is not ladylike and immediately puts a smile on my face.

"Cam. Are you afraid of horses?"

"Not afraid, I've just never had the opportunity to get close enough to one to make an acquaintance."

"We will be rectifying that little issue." She twirls her finger in the air as if that seals the deal. "Let's head back. We've got a sink to fix."

"I interrupted your story. Sorry." I watch as she cocks her head to match Max's.

"You know, I think I know what I need to do. Thanks for listening. I find that when people talk through their problems, they often find they've known the answer all along."

This time she is the one offering me the hand up. I accept it. She's stronger than she looks. She gives a swift pull, and I plow into her, wrapping my arm around her back, so we both don't fall. Evie doesn't back away, and I find myself very close to those beautiful eyes and lips.

"Tree in the face," I blurt out before taking a giant step back. Laughter looks good on her.

We chat comfortably as we drive to her house. I see it the moment we turn onto her street. The black 4Runner from the church is in her driveway.

Nine

Everly

"Evie? Are you expecting company?"

My heart sinks a little at Cam's question. "No, why?"

"There's a black SUV in your driveway."

Scott? What is he doing here? Gravel lets me know we've arrived. I grab my pack at my feet and hop out of the truck. Misjudging the distance to the ground, I stumble. Cam is beside me in an instant, steadying me. I hear my screen door open.

"Where have you been?" Scott's words are harsh. The steel in his clipped words makes me freeze, unable to move forward. His feet fall heavily on the eight steps down to me as he moves our direction. 'Our' direction. Cam slowly releases my arm but doesn't move away.

"Hey, Scott! What brings you by this afternoon?" Every word is forced. He stops in front of us, and, like the heat from a recently opened oven door, I can feel the tension roll over me. Max lets out a low, menacing growl from the truck.

"I'm Cameron Boyd."

Thank the Lord one of us can speak.

"Scott Hassen." The pause is longer than it should be. I assume they shake hands. "Why didn't you take your phone?"

I'm completely taken aback, both by his tone and the fact I haven't missed the phone that's always on my person.

"You left it on the charger next to your house keys. You didn't even lock up, Evie."

Now I'm getting irritated. Scott has never spoken to me this way. It feels almost possessive, and I don't like it. I lift my chin and my eyebrow but refuse to play into whatever game he's started.

"What brings you by?" My words are overly sweet; my breathing is controlled. Someone's feet shuffle, but I can't tell whom I've made nervous until I hear the familiar deep intake of breath and slow release. I've never challenged Scott like this, and I've made him uncomfortable.

"It's your mom. Nurse Darla called me after she couldn't reach you."

I feel Cam's hand lightly touch the small of my back, and it grounds me. It also helps me focus.

"Cam," I turn and realize he is closer than I first

thought. He steps back. "Thank you for fixing my gutter. Please send me a bill." I'm not sure why I don't mention having a lovely time or thank him for his listening ear.

"Right. No problem. I'll make an appointment to fix your sink later this week. Nice to meet you, Scott."

He is gone before I can amend my thoughtlessness. I've hurt him, brushed him off. When the truck has pulled out, I turn and take my anger and frustration out on Scott.

"Seriously, Scott? Where do you get off talking to me like I'm a child? I'm not, you know." I stomp my foot and hear a snicker. "And you're not my keeper." My harsh words burn my lips. I struggle to open my cane and jerk my arm back when Scott reaches to assist me. I'm mad. I'm frustrated. I'm worried.

I quickly change clothes inside the house, not caring that Scott is standing in the kitchen waiting. I brush my hair and splash water on my face, then rebrush damp tendrils up into a ponytail. My feet wear cement shoes as I trudge from the bathroom. Every step is a chore. I need to apologize. I fill my lungs with air.

"I'm sorry."

"I'm sorry." Our words are in unison, or more like harmony, but both in perfect timing.

"Scott," Before I can finish, I feel his arms around

me, trapping my own against him. I melt into his familiarity. He is still my rock. "What happened?"

"She fell at some point this morning and hit her head. She's at Watauga Medical Center." He releases his hold, but his touch doesn't leave me. "I was worried about you."

I nod but don't respond.

"Gutter?"

It takes me a minute to follow his train of thought. Mine is on my mom. His is obviously on Cam.

"Will you take me to see her?" I can only focus on this one thing right now and choose to ignore his question.

"Of course."

He grabs my phone and keys, placing the phone in its proper pocket. The key turns in the lock before I feel pressure on my backpack. He's also stored my keys in their familiar spot on my bag. This is how we roll. We work well together.

We ride in silence. My mind drifts from what might have happened with Mom to the food I've left in the backpack in Cam's truck, and I wonder if he'll think to take it inside and wash out my containers.

"Do you want me to go in with you?"

Scott's question is courteous, not controlling, and it soothes my anxious nerves. I'm confident with my cane in familiar surroundings, but I've never been to this hospital or any hospital outside of a few ER visits. Anxiety wins over independence.

"Yes, please." I reach over, placing my hand on the edge of his seat. "I'm sorry I didn't have my phone, and I'm sorry for how I spoke to you."

He lays his hand on top of mine and folds his fingers into my palm.

"You don't owe me an explanation."

I don't unfurl my cane when he opens my door. He offers his arm, and I take it, momentarily leaning my head into his soft shoulder. It's nothing like Cam's. My mind wanders to what now seems like eons ago. When Cam had nearly bowled me over, he'd held me just long enough for me to know—he likes me, too. I trip over the curb and hold tighter to Scott's arm.

"Tree in the face," I quip, a smile crossing my face.

"Oh, sorry about that. I was reading the directional sign. Wait, what?"

"Nothing." I pat his arm much like I do Max's head and almost say 'good boy' but restrain myself.

Getting to Mom's room isn't easy, even for a seeing person. Scott's knuckles rap on the wooden door.

"Come in." Mom's voice is raspy, quiet.

"Hi, Mrs. Sherman. I brought you your favorite

person. Thought it might cheer you up."

I almost laugh, but her tender response catches me off guard. No fake 'darling' comes before or after she speaks my name in a hushed tone. My name floats to me on butterfly wings, momentarily remaining before it is gone. Scott removes my hand from his arm and places it on the railing at the side of mom's bed. My mom's aging one immediately covers it.

"Scott, darling, would you please put this bedrail down so Evie can sit up here with me?"

He does as she asks, adjusting the blankets and my mom's legs before assisting me up. I pull my legs under me, much like I did as a child sitting on her bed watching her get ready for an evening out.

"I'll get you a cup of coffee."

His footsteps fade into the distance, and I feel utterly alone until Mom's hand touches my knee. Her finger moves back and forth over the fabric of my jeans.

"You look nice."

It's the first compliment she's given me in a long time, and I struggle to believe her.

"What happened?" My question is curt with a hint of concern.

"I'm not certain. I was getting dressed, then I woke up, and here I am." Air moves in front of me, and I guess she has gestured to the room.

We sit, silent, her finger breaking down the blue fibers. I feel a tug in my heart and know the Holy Spirit is prompting me to tell Mom about church on Sunday.

"Mom?" She doesn't respond verbally, but her finger stills. "I've been mad at you for a long time." Her gentle laugh tells me this isn't news to her. It bolsters my courage. "At church on Sunday, the pastor...."

For the next hour, I share my heart. Words and thoughts, feelings and hurts, all pour out of me like my tears. When I finish, I have nothing left in me. At some point, Mom has placed the hospital tissue box near me. The fine-grade sandpaper has scraped off more than tears.

"Everly Peabody," Mom's hand grips my knee, "I love you, and I am so, so sorry." It is a desperate whisper, and the most gut-wrenching sob I have ever heard follows.

Without thought, I lean forward, my head landing near her hip. Her hand touches my head, and I wonder if this is what Max experiences. It is comforting and uncomfortable at the same time. I can't recall when my mother has ever stroked my hair; brushed it out of my face, maybe, but not like this. I melt into the bed, into her, and relax, allowing my tears to flow.

A nurse interrupts us. "How are you feeling?" She doesn't seem concerned or surprised at our odd arrangement.

"Fine," my mother whispers, her voice now hoarse.

Beeps and sounds I do not recognize begin to fill the room. I listen to the soft padding of the nurse's feet as she moves around. Having something to focus on allows me to get control of my breathing, my emotions.

"All done here. Use your call button if you need anything. Is that nice young man outside your beau?" Neither Mom nor I speak. Mr. Wonderful wouldn't be allowed to visit, so I guess she means Scott.

"Scott?" I say his name louder than intended. I've forgotten all about him.

"You called?"

He is beside me in a moment and assists me off Mom's bed. He has probably heard the entire conversation, but I doubt he learned any new revelations. I've hashed over past hurts with him more times than I care to remember. He hands me a cup.

"It's cold, but it's black."

"Thanks." I take a sip and nearly gag. Mom laughs. It sounds good.

"Scott, would you give us a few more minutes?" Mom's voice is tender.

"Of course." He lightly touches my arm. "I'll run

to Dunkin for real coffee and grab your favorite while I'm there. I heard your stomach growl from the hallway."

I nod but don't respond. Wood scrapes the floor as Scott moves a chair over for me so I can sit.

"Thanks," is all I can manage. When I'm settled, and Scott is gone, I hear my mother adjust herself in the bed.

"I'd like to talk about this if you're willing."

Mom's words are laced with something akin to fear. This is hard for her. I swallow and heed the Spirit's nudging. I choose to show grace.

"Yes." My answer is affirmative; my tone invites her to continue.

"I'm so sorry, Everly." I hear sandpaper take another layer of cardboard off the edge of the box. "I thought I was doing the right thing by making you independent. I guess I just went about it the wrong way."

I breathe deeply through my nose, keeping my lips tightly closed since my brain is screaming, 'Ya' think?' I feel the familiar nudge of the Holy Spirit reminding me to be gracious.

"Your father was blind."

I hear her words, but it is as if they are coming from the far end of a tunnel. She's never spoken of him.

"His name was Frank, and he was my first love. He was already blind when I met him." She gently blows her nose, and it sounds as if the effort has tired her.

"I was seventeen, hated my life, and was ready for adventure. He was twenty, ran the sound system for a band, and offered me an opportunity I couldn't refuse. I traveled with his group for a year, doing odd jobs to earn my keep, until..." She pauses just long enough to let me know this is difficult for her. "Until I found out I was pregnant with you."

It feels like too much to take in, but I crave more.

"I intentionally didn't get on the bus after the next gig. He probably didn't realize I was missing until the following morning." Her next words are so quiet, I almost miss them. "I did it for you, Everly. I had to get you away from the drinking, the drugs; it was no place to raise a child."

I wonder if she's fallen asleep. Her breathing has slowed, and she is still. I'm about to stand and locate a restroom when I hear her begin again.

"I tried to figure out how to make enough money to support us, but I had no one to watch you. The little I'd saved while waitressing before you were born only lasted a short time. So, I did what I had to do. I got married."

It's as if scales are being lifted from my eyes. I'm seeing for the first time why my mom made certain choices.

"Bill, he was a good man. He hadn't wanted children but was good to us. Do you remember riding cross-country in the cab of his tractor-trailer?" Her voice sounds like sweet memories. "You were probably too little. We saw the Pacific to the Atlantic through the windshield, even had some fun, but a toddler needs room to roam, and you still weren't yet walking at three-years-old. So, I asked him to take a local route and settle down. He met me halfway. He set me up in a little apartment and gave me my freedom." Her intake of breath is deep, cleansing, as if she, too, is finding healing in her words.

"Next was Simon the Shyster." Her laugh isn't genuine; hurt taints the sound. "I thought we were married, but his other wives, yes plural, disagreed. I'm just thankful he didn't hurt you."

I wonder if that means he hurt her, but I don't ask.

"Simon had one good trait. He was a gift-giver. I took every piece of jewelry and pawned it, giving us enough money to move. Again."

"Larry, you know well. I know you didn't enjoy going to so many different schools with all his job transfers."

I shrug my shoulders. This is Mom's story, and I'm interested in hearing it.

"When Larry died, I couldn't afford the mortgage on the house. I got a job at the grocery down the street. I had no education or worthwhile job history.

It's a marvel they hired me at all until I learned that Tom, the store owner, liked me. He was married but kept us in our home."

What Mom hasn't said is revealing and churns my stomach. I remember coming home from school and seeing a creepy bald guy leaving our house.

"When I couldn't take it anymore, we set off on another adventure. Ohio seemed as good a place as any. It was the first place you made friends, and I was jealous."

My mouth opens to say something, anything, but nothing comes out.

"Evie, could you get some water for me, please?"

As usual, she gives me no instructions. I think through where water might be and find a table near her head. On top is a plastic cup with a thick bendy straw. I twirl the cup and realize it is full of liquid with ice. She drinks from it but never lifts her arms to take it. I brush off the thought that she doesn't want to touch me and focus more on my concern for her lack of strength. She begins again when I sit back in the chair.

"Phil and I didn't make it a year, but he gave me a huge gift by teaching me how to use the computer. I got my office job at Harris Trucking, and the rest is history."

"Why didn't you tell me this sooner, Mom?" Confusion wars with anger.

"You weren't ready to hear it."

Pain seeps from her words, and I know she's right.

"What now?" It has taken me several moments to get those words out. I'm not sure I want to know the answer.

"I'm dying, Everly."

There is resignation in those few words. I know it is inevitable, just like she knows.

"This fall may have shortened my days."

She deeply exhales as if she has made a decision but isn't happy about it.

"May I give you some advice?"

"Yes." Surprisingly, I mean it.

"Don't marry for convenience, comfort, or casual love. Marry someone because you can't live another day without him, and he makes you a better version of yourself. Fall in love, deeply, passionately, and fully. Never settle for less than God's best for you."

Out of that entire speech, I laser focus on one thing.

"God?" It is all I can manage.

This time mom's laughter is light, bright, and fills my heart with hope.

"Yes, Everly. You aren't the only one to find God. I just took a little longer."

Ten

Cam

Max and I ride home in silence except for the bursts of breath coming from my mouth and the sound my hand makes on the steering wheel each time it and my hand connects. My emotions are all over the place: She's unbelievable! Did I misinterpret something? Scott needs to be knocked down a peg. What did I do wrong?

Self-doubt wins. I get all the way home before I realize I have nothing to eat. I can either call for a pizza, or head to Food Lion and get a frozen one. I open my fridge and realize groceries are probably a better choice, but I can't do people right now.

I give my address and place my order--one large, all the meats, extra cheese, and one small cheese since the sausage sometimes upsets Max's stomach. I add an order of buffalo wings for tomorrow and whatever the dessert thing is they carry.

Thankfully, football is on. Max is already curled

up on the sofa waiting for me. We stuff ourselves with slice after slice. As I put the leftovers away, I hear Max whining at the door to go out. This is the first night since college that he and I haven't sat on the porch and listened to the night sounds.

"Sorry, boy." I attach the leash to his collar and follow the lights lining my driveway. He does his business and heads back in without my prompting. "You're as upset as I am, aren't you?" Mournful eyes look up and a deep sigh escapes before he plops on his bed. He doesn't even turn around three times before finding just the right position. He's resigned himself to misery. Just like me.

I stare at myself with self-loathing as I brush my teeth. Water and toothpaste swirl in the sink, finally going down the drain. Philippians 4:6-7 come to mind. I need the peace of God to guard my heart and mind. I look at my reflection in the mirror and know God is reminding me to trust Him.

Like I did as a child, I kneel before the chair my grandfather once occupied. I cry out to God, sharing my hurts, fears, disappointments, and the physical pain that is squeezing my heart. I can't remember the last time I cried. It is healing. The peace I experience after fully giving my problem to God is like no other. The pain subsides but does not fully leave. Yet, it serves as a reminder to keep my focus on Christ, not on those things I have just laid at His feet. When I stand, I know I have given it to Him completely.

The heaviness that weighed on me lifts a little more with each passing day. It takes everything within me not to show up at her house or just drive by to see if I might get a glimpse of her. Instead, I've spent time on something completely surprising-- I've looked into what it would take to become a licensed independent contractor.

Evie's question from our walk has burrowed into the recesses of my mind. Every evening after work, I've noticed something new in the home my grandfather built. My eyes catch details I didn't see before, such as how he did things, not to save money, but to make the home aesthetically pleasing, and built to last.

I've spent two nights in the workshop taking inventory of the tools he handed down to me. Even Max seems to share my excitement. He sits beside me on the deck watching YouTube videos on my phone with me after the stars come out.

I need a catchy business name and mull over several: Cam's Contractor Services, Boyd's Builders, and a few others, but nothing hits me just right. I can't fill out the paperwork for my license until I have a name.

On Thursday after work, I stop at the local hardware store, something I haven't done since my grandfather was alive.

"Cam, is that you?" Mr. Kinder shuffles my direction, hand outstretched.

I take his work-worn hand in mine and feel an instant connection.

"Yes, sir. It's been a while. How are you?"

"Son, I'm 87 years old, how do you think I am?" He laughs then coughs, pulling a white hanky from his back pocket to wipe his mouth. "What brings you in? Or should I be asking, what kept you away?"

He may be old, but he doesn't miss a thing.

"Well, sir, I came to ask your advice."

"Sounds like we need coffee."

He doesn't ask. He turns and maneuvers between boxes and crates into the backroom I remember well. He and my grandfather would sit and talk for hours while I earned a quarter sorting nails, screws, nuts, and bolts into small jars.

My heart already feels lighter after talking to Mr. Kinder for an hour. I think back to what Evie said after she shared her heart with me--'I find that when people talk through their problems, they often find they've known the answer all along.' She is right. I have known the answer. Now I just need to wait on the Lord.

Eleven

Everly

I haven't heard from Cam all week. I don't have his phone number. He knows where I live, but I expect I've wounded him so profoundly that he won't be coming back. I'm dreading work tonight. How can I possibly host a show on a topic on which I am a complete failure?

Ginger's text ringtone pulls me from my dreary thoughts.

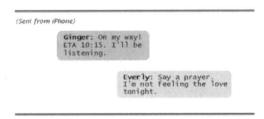

(Sent from iPhone)

Ginger: On my way! ETA 10:15. I'll be listening.

Everly: Say a prayer. I'm not feeling the love tonight.

I attach the picture of Cam and send it.

(Sent from iPhone)

Ginger: Is that Cam?

Everly: Yes. I haven't heard from him all week. I really hurt him.

Ginger: God knows, Evie. Put that winning smile on your face for now, and we'll drown our sorrows with Oreos and Mint Chocolate Chip tonight after I pick you up.

Securing my phone in my bag, I lock up and head down to meet the Uber taking me to work.

"It's always a beautiful Friday night in Blowing Rock, North Carolina. You're listening to JOY radio with host Everly Johnson. We're ready for our first caller. Welcome, Megan. You're on the air. What brings joy into your life today?"

"Hi, Everly! So, I'm getting married."

Images of a 1980's Valley Girl come to mind. "Congratulations. Do you want to ask a question or are you just announcing the happy news?"

"Well, actually, I have a question. It's like this, I'm having second thoughts. What if I'm not ready? What if he isn't the one?"

My mom's advice floods my mind, and I repeat it nearly word for word without thought. "I think you should marry because you can't live another day without that person. Marriage isn't for convenience, comfort, or casual love. Your future spouse should make you a better version of yourself."

"What if I'm not that kind of person for him?" Gone is Valley Girl; now it is just a girl, one who is hurting.

"Someone recently told me God can use people who are willing to admit they don't measure up. Megan, I know you want me to give you the answer, but this is something only you, your fiancé, and God can work out." I hear a sniff.

"Megan, thank you for calling in. Here's a song by The Afters, *Fear No More*, that I think will minister to your heart." I press play and remove my headset before I can hear what Scott has started to say.

My heart physically aches for Cam. We spent only a short time together, but I know he is the one for me. I press the heels of my hands into my eyes to stay the tears I feel rising.

"God, help me." I cry out in a whisper.

Tap, tap, tap. I replace my headphone and hear Walt's frantic voice telling Scott to stop before he breaks the glass.

"Everly! 3, 2, 1."

"I'm so glad you could join us..." I can't find the caller's name, so leave it at that.

"Hi, Everly." The caller reminds me of Eeyore.

I muddle through this call, then another, then

another, then another. The night drags on, and I struggle to stay upbeat. I play a song and remove my headset, needing a break, and hear the door to the studio open.

"Wow, Everly." It isn't Scott's voice, but rather his dad's that I hear.

This isn't a social call. As the owner of the station, I've never known him to stop in.

"Hi, Mr. Hassen." My voice shakes.

"Everly, can I give you some fatherly advice?" He continues at my nod. "Don't let whatever is going on between you and my son affect you. Now for some owner of the station advice. Don't let whatever is going on between you and my station manager affect your job." His words are gentle but firm. "Do you understand?"

"I do, sir. Thank you." I mean it; he has given me a gift. I pick up my headset. "Putting on a new frame of mind right now, sir."

The rest of the calls flow much more smoothly. There are moments of genuine connection with several callers, and I feel I've got my groove back. The night is over before I know it.

"Thank you for inviting me into your home this Friday evening. We here at JOY radio pray your weekend is full of joyous encounters. Remember to choose joy in every circumstance. Until next week, this is Everly Johnson, your Christian Singles Advice

Host at WJOY radio, Blowing Rock, NC."

"Ready to go?" At Ginger's words, I squeal and open my arms for the hug I know I am about to receive.

"I'm so glad you came down." I grab my pack and enfold my arm in hers.

"Hi, Scott. Bye, Scott," she sings over her shoulder between us.

"Bye, ladies. I don't have enough bail money for two, so you'll need to choose who gets out." Scott calls to our backs as we giggle our way out of the building.

"I already stopped at Food Lion. We've got everything we need for a girls' weekend in."

Ginger's car has that new car smell.

"Did you get a new car?" I feel the door panel, wondering if anything feels different.

"Nope, just cleaned this one. There's this really cute guy at our local car wash, so I've been going once a month. This time I splurged on the deluxe."

Ginger is a full-figured girl with dark brown hair. I know this because she reminds me often. She doesn't date, or at least she never tells me about any, and we share everything.

"What's on the agenda?"

I feel like she's changing the subject, but I know Ginger is a details girl. She likes to know when, where, who, what, and how all in advance. She doesn't usually do spur-of-the-moment well, which is one reason I'm surprised she popped down this weekend. It's about an eight-hour drive from Ohio, which means she took a half day off from work.

"Well, I haven't had much time to think about it. Is there anything special you'd like to do while you're here?"

She hesitates only for a moment. "Eat!"

We both laugh, and I know that besides all the sugar she has bought, we'll be hitting up her favorite restaurants in town this weekend.

If I have to eat another Oreo, I might gag. I don't even want to know how many calories are in those things. This is one time I'm thankful they don't put braille on packaging. I pull on my dress for church and have to hook the wide belt one hole bigger than usual. Not cool.

We stayed up way too late and ate far too much. Like old times, we talked of boys, our futures, and sprinkled in a healthy dose of Hallmark.

"Evie, do you have black flats? Somehow I packed my blue pair by mistake and they look awful with this dress!" I hear her call from the guest room.

I feel the tags on my shoes until I find the one labeled BK for black. BL is blue, BR is brown.

"Try these. I think I've only worn them once."

"Perfect! Thanks!" I hear her toss them on the floor and slide them on. "Ready?"

I take a final sip of coffee and rinse our mugs before heading out to her car.

We arrive early yet still sit near the back to people watch; one of her favorite pastimes. She describes outlandish hairstyles, flashy outfits, and audacious jewelry. We giggle, and I realize paying attention to the sermon will be like college days during chapel. I'm just thankful we won't receive demerits for our actions.

"Oh my gosh, Evie. It's him!" Her words, meant to be a whisper, are super loud. The person beside me gives an exaggerated sigh.

"Who?" I whisper back much more quietly.

"He is way cuter than his picture."

"Who?" I ask a little more forcefully.

"Cam."

"Cam?" I'm trying to put the pieces together. Where did she see a picture, and what is he doing here?

"Yes, silly. You texted his picture to me Friday. Remember?" I nod. "You didn't tell me he attended church here."

"Hello, ladies." Scott leans over the back row between us. "No jail time?"

"We still have opportunities. I'm staying another day." Ginger's voice holds a hint of flirtatiousness.

"Is that so? Would you ladies care for a picnic lunch at Bass Lake? I'll stop and get BBQ."

Ginger has turned in her seat so far she's practically on top of me. Her leg is bouncing, and I know what that means; she's struggling with changing plans we've already made but desperately wants to go.

"It's up to you, Ginger. You know I'm always game for anything, especially if Scott's buying."

She squirms, and I hear a tiny sound coming from her as if she's gearing up to say something, but it won't come out.

"Yes." Her answer comes out in a whoosh.

Scott laughs. "Alrighty then. I'll meet you guys near the first bench around noon."

"We'll bring dessert," I offer. I don't want those Oreos in my house after she's gone. The music starts, and Ginger turns in her seat.

"I can't believe I just did that." Ginger's words are breathy.

"I'm glad you did. We'll have a good time." It dawns on me that I'm entirely comfortable with this situation, and I smile, knowing Scott and I can still be friends. Ginger has forgotten about Cam, but I haven't. It takes effort to focus on the worship song.

"Ginger, seriously, it's a picnic!" Exasperation coats my words, and I feel my jaw clench. She's changed clothes three times. I've thrown on yoga pants, a t-shirt, and a hoodie.

"How do I look," she asks again.

"Perfect. Let's go."

"You're no fun," she giggles, but there is a hint of hurt in her words.

"Ginger, you could wear sackcloth and look good, so I know I'm telling you the truth. Whatever you finally decided to wear is perfect."

"Thanks, Evie."

All weekend we've sounded like teenage girls talking about our crushes. I have no idea if Scott likes Ginger or not, and I certainly don't want to see either of my friends get hurt, but I'll do whatever it takes to make sure this is a memorable day for Ginger.

"The parking spaces are all full. I'm going to need to be creative. Oh, wait, someone's pulling out." We park and walk down the steps where Ginger spots Scott. "He's waving!" Ginger's words hold excitement and possibility.

"Wondered if you guys had gotten lost." Scott has a smile in his tone.

"You know me, couldn't figure out what to wear."

I joke as I pull my hoodie over my ponytail. Scott laughs, knowing full well I could go on a vacation for a week with only my backpack. Clothes have never mattered to me.

"Mmm, smells good! I'm starving." Ginger helps me to the edge of the blanket and sits.

"Have you had a good visit, Ginger?" Scott's question is genuine.

Ginger hands a paper plate full of food to me as she starts in on how much we ate. Scott says a quick prayer before we all dig in. Woodlands is some of the best BBQ around, and I always enjoy their hushpuppies.

"What in the...Evie!"

Scott's panicked words and Ginger's scream make me instinctively cover my head and curl up into a ball. The force that hits me knocks me over, my arms failing to stop me from rolling. I hear my scream gurgling from the depths, but nothing comes out because I can't breathe.

"Max! Max! Off! I'm so sorry. Are you okay, miss?" Even out of breath, I'd recognize that voice anywhere. I reach up and pull my hoodie from my head, and smile.

"Hey there, Max. How's my good boy?" Max is now beside me. I sit up and wrap my arms around his barrel chest.

"Evie?"

"Hey, Cam." I hope he can hear me; fur still surrounds my face.

"Scott, right? Cameron Boyd. We met the other day at Evie's. I fixed the gutter?"

"Right! Looks good. This is Ginger," I hear the faint sounds of greetings, "and you know Evie."

I still don't move.

"Cam, we have plenty of food; why don't you join us?"

If I could glare at Ginger, I would. What is she doing?

"No, that's okay."

"No, really, if you don't want BBQ, please at least have a few Oreos. I'm getting fat."

"You're not fat."

My head pops up at Scott's quiet words to Ginger.

"You have no idea what you're talking about." Ginger jokes back.

"Um, you're sitting on me. I think I have some idea."

Scott laughs, and I hear Ginger scootch away. She has some serious explaining to do.

"Your dog, Max is it? He can be a little intimidating at breakneck speed." Ginger giggles nervously.

"Sorry about that. We got out of the car, and I didn't even get his leash on before he caught a scent and barreled down the hill and straight to," he pauses just a fraction of a moment, "Evie."

"Good choice in women," Scott murmurs under his breath.

"Yeah."

I don't think Cam has meant to say this out loud. He clears his throat.

"We need to get going." Max growls.

"I think Max disagrees. Join us, please. Then we'll all take a hike together." Scott surprises me with his sincere offer.

Cam entertains us with Max stories while Max licks our plates clean before we pack up and throw away our trash. Max stays by my side, causing Cam to walk with me. Ginger and Scott are having a conversation behind us and seem to be doing just fine on their own.

"I want to apologize for my behavior on Monday. It was wrong of me to brush you off so casually, and I feel horrible." I turn to him, hoping he sees the sincerity in my face.

"You are a mystery to me, Evie."

His quiet words give me no indication if he has forgiven me or not.

"What's with those two?"

"What?"

"Scott and Ginger." He must have leaned in to

whisper because Max bumps into my leg. "She was literally in his lap." He laughs.

I carefully listen before I speak to see how far behind us they are and judge whether or not they can hear our conversation.

"Until this weekend, I had no idea she liked him, but it appears to be mutual."

"Are you okay with that?"

He's more of a detective than I've given him credit for and has picked up on some clues through observation only.

"I am," I say with all sincerity. "The three of us have been friends since college, but Scott has never been more than that to me." Cam takes a deep breath and I continue. "So, can you forgive me?" I can't let it go. It is gnawing at me, and I'm not too fond of this feeling.

"I'm thinking about it."

There is a slight bit of teasing, and I take that as a good sign. "Well, don't think too long."

Ginger leaves Monday, and texts when she arrives home before nightfall. Having her here was just what I needed, and exactly what she wanted. She and Scott went out for breakfast before she got on the road, then she called and talked with me for three of the eight hours' drive home. When we hung up, my phone rang and it was Scott and I heard the same story again, only he was able to compress it into fifteen minutes.

All week long I work to be happy for them, even as my own heart aches. I still haven't heard from Cam. I guess I am hoping it will be a happily-ever-after for me, too. Ginger and Scott sure seem to be headed in that direction.

It's Thursday night and I'm headed to bed when I receive a text alert on my phone. I don't recognize the number, but I know who it is. The text contains a single word.

(Sent from iPhone)

Cam: Forgiven.

My heart is relieved, and my soul feels peace for the first time in too long.

(Sent from iPhone)

Everly: About time...

Everly: Thank you.

"What a pleasure it has been to be with you this evening. This will be our last call of the night. Welcome, Max, I'm so glad you could join us tonight. What brings joy into your life this evening?"

"Hi, Everly."

I know his voice instantly. Elation and fear crowd my rational thoughts.

"What brings you joy?" My throat constricts, and I struggle to get the canned words out.

"I figured out a mystery today."

I decide to play along. "Agatha Christie style?" I ask casually, my throat loosening some.

"More Sherlock Holmes; elementary deductions."

"Ah, 'you see, but you do not observe' kind of deductions? And how does solving this mystery bring you joy?"

"Because it opened my eyes to the only thing that really matters in life. Sort of like a tree in the face kind of moment." I laugh and cover my mouth with my hand. "I've met this girl, this ray of sunshine."

My heart melts at the endearment. "Is there anything special you'd like to share about her?"

"She's amazing. She's hardworking and caring. She makes me laugh over ridiculous things. She's a great listener, makes a mean chicken salad sandwich, and is adventurous. Oh, and she likes my dog."

"She sounds... "

He interrupts me. "Perfect. Absolutely perfect."

"Well, Max, it sounds like you found a real gem. We're almost out of time, but is there anything you'd like to say to Miss Perfect on the air?"

"I love you, Evie."

I can't breathe. Scott is frantically tapping in my headphones. Thankfully my practiced words flow from memory.

"Thank you for inviting me into your home this Friday evening. We here at JOY radio pray your weekend is full of joyous encounters. Remember to choose joy in every circumstance. Until next week, this is Everly Johnson, your Christian Singles Advice Host at WJOY radio, Blowing Rock, NC."

My headphones are off, my head buried in my hands. He loves me. The studio door opens. A deep sigh originates from my left before something heavy presses down on my knee. Warm fur pushes against my hands.

"Max?" Both paws are on my shoulders, causing my chair to topple with the weight. "Off." My command is gentle, but he immediately obeys.

"I've never been able to get him to obey that one."

Cam takes my hand and gently pulls me to him. My heart is keeping rhythm with the beat of the song playing overhead.

"How..." My breath catches in my throat as he pulls my hand to his mouth and kisses my fingers before releasing it and placing his hands on my tear-stained face.

I feel his warm breath on my cool cheeks as he kisses each one before his lips gently brush my lips. I can't tell if the moan is from me or Max. It's my first real kiss and it is heavenly. Mom's words rush in, 'Evie, fall in love, deeply, passionately, and fully. And, never settle for less than God's best for you.'

For the first time in my life, I know my mom is right.

The End

ACKNOWLEDGEMENT

It is pure joy writing for fun and not a deadline. Months before the release date set by the You Are On The Air series, I had already written "The End."

Lisa Prysock, Chautona Havig, Marlene Bierworth, and the other authors in the *You Are On The Air* series took me in and provided encouragement as I challenged myself to move from Historical to Contemporary Fiction. You'll want to see what fun stories these ladies have coming up by visiting my website. You'll find a list of all twenty-six books, along with their release dates.

http://heidimcgill822089357.wordpress.com/

Being new to Contemporary Fiction meant I didn't have a reader base. A special thank you to my Historical Reader Insiders, who stepped out of their traditional genre and let me know this book is good...and funny...and worth the read. You are amazing friends.

Thanks also go out to two friends who share my

disability: Amy Bovaird provided connections with other visually impaired authors, bloggers, and podcasters who jumped on board in promoting the book during February, which is Low Vision Awareness Month. Ann Harrison, a communications expert, helped ensure everything regarding Everly's job in radio was plausible and as accurate as possible.

Davida Sabine, Stephanie Brank Leupp, Sheri Sweatman, and Cindi Nipper provided editorial corrections. These ladies are gems.

There are not enough words to thank my precious friend, Danica Lohmeyer, tech geek extraordinaire. Danica spent hours formatting to create an accessible document that allows assistive technologies such as screen readers and Braille devices to read the book for those with visual impairment.

It is always appropriate to thank my Savior. As a Christ-follower, my greatest desire is to honor Him in all I do.

Heidi

ABOUT THE AUTHOR

Heidi Gray Mcgill

Heidi is an optimist who chooses to find the silver lining in life's clouds of doubt. This plays out in her writing. Her ability to seamlessly weave scripture into the lives of her characters will uplift and en-  courage you, while her masterful storytelling will keep you turning page after page and wishing for more.

Heidi lives with her husband of thirty years near Charlotte, NC. When she isn't writing, you will find her outside playing with her two grandsons, walking, scrapbooking, reading, cooking, traveling, or finding an excuse to have an outing with a girlfriend.

BOOKS BY THIS AUTHOR

Desire Of My Heart, Book 1, Discerning God's Best Series

Aging out of the orphanage leaves Rachel with few options. She refuses an arranged marriage and orchestrates a narrow escape, dragging her younger brother, Charlie, with her into an unforeseeable future with a man she doesn't know but who needs her as much as she needs him.

An uplifting, wholesome, and inspirational book that will keep you engaged to the very end.

With All My Heart, Book 2 Discerning God's Best Series

Overcoming lifelong rejection is not what keeps Singing Bird from loving, but it keeps her accepting love.

Hiding from those who seek to do her harm, Singing

Bird and Little Sun must survive on the land and their own sheer grit. The two seek shelter in the only place Singing Bird has ever felt welcomed, appreciated, and protected. Only, in doing so, she places herself near the one man she has tried to forget.

NEXT IN THE SERIES

Emma Jane Riley, hell-bent on saving her family's tiny AM station in Why Me, WY, thinks she's struck gold when she hires famous air personality from LA, Bobby Ringo. Turns out, Ringo was easy to hire for a reason. Unbeknownst to Emma Jane, he's recovering from a heartbreak and has let his drinking get out of hand. He hopes Why Me is the place he can gather up his wits and his heart...away from the spotlight.

Emma Jane worries his boozing and big city ways won't sit well with the folks in Why Me and wants out of the deal. But when Ringo hands out some amazingly intuitive, Biblical advice on-air, the town starts warming up to him...until he tells the local lovesick cowboys to lose in their upcoming rodeo finals. The town is in an uproar. Will the boys throw their rides, or won't they? And how do the girls at the heart of the conflict feel about this advice? Is it romantic or foolish? Poor Emma Jane wants to kill Ringo for the controversy...but instead finds he's stealing her heart.

Get your copy and see all the books in the series by visiting: https://heidimcgill822089357. wordpress.com/you-are-on-the-air/

Made in the USA
Monee, IL
25 May 2022

97037268R00088